ASQ's Pocket Guide Series

Machine Learning Fundamentals

By Nicole Radziwill

Quality Press
Milwaukee, Wisconsin

Machine Learning Fundamentals
Nicole Radziwill
American Society for Quality, Quality Press, Milwaukee 53203

Publisher's Cataloging-in-Publication Data
Names: Radziwill, Nicole M., 1976, author.
Title: Machine learning fundamentals / Nicole Radziwill.
Series: ASQ's Pocket Guide Series
Description: Includes bibliographical references. | Milwaukee, WI: Quality Press, 2026.
Identifiers: LCCN: 2026934722 | ISBN: 9781636942384 (paperback) | 9781636942391 (pdf) | 9781636942407 (epub)
Subjects: LCSH Machine learning. | BISAC COMPUTERS / Data Science / Machine Learning | COMPUTERS / Artificial Intelligence / General | TECHNOLOGY & ENGINEERING / Automation | TECHNOLOGY & ENGINEERING / Manufacturing
Classification: LCC Q325.5 .R33 2026 | DDC 006.31--d23

ASQ advances individual, organizational, and community excellence worldwide through learning, quality improvement, and knowledge exchange.

Bookstores, wholesalers, schools, libraries, businesses, and organizations: Quality Press books are available at quantity discounts for bulk purchases for business, trade, or educational uses. For more information, please contact Quality Press at 800-248-1946 or books@asq.org.

To place orders or browse the selection of all Quality Press titles, visit our website at: http://www.asq.org/quality-press.

30 29 28 27 26 LS 7 6 5 4 3 2 1

Quality Press
600 N. Plankinton Ave.
Milwaukee, WI 53203-2914
Email: books@asq.org

Table of Contents

Acronyms

AI—Artificial Intelligence

API—Applicable Programming Interface

AUC—Area Under the Curve

CER—Character Error Rate

CNN—Convolutional Neural Network

CRM—Customer Relationship Management

CTQ—Critical to Quality

FMI—Fowlkes-Mallows Index

FN—False Negative

FP—False Positive

GMM—Gaussian Mixture Models

HDBSCAN—Hierarchical Density-Based Spatial Clustering of Applications with Noise

HMM—Hidden Markov Models

IQR—Interquartile Range

JKK—*Ji kotei kanketsu* (Own Process Ownership)

LLM—Large Language Model

LOF—Local Outlier Factor

LSTM—Long Short-Term Memory

MAE—Mean Absolute Error

MCC—Matthew Correlation Coefficient

ML—Machine Learning

MLOps—Machine Learning Operations

MSE—Mean Squared Error

NLP—Natural Language Processing

OOB—Out-of-Bag

PCA—Principal Component Analysis

PDCA—Plan-Do-Check-Act

PDSA—Plan-Do-Study-Act

POS—Point of Sale

RMSE—Root Mean Squared Error

ROC—Receiver Operating Characteristic

SHAP—SHapley Additive exPlanations

SIPOC—Suppliers, Inputs, Process, Outputs, Customers

SMOTE—Synthetic Minority Oversampling Technique

SoPK—System of Profound Knowledge (Deming)

SVM—Support Vector Machine

TF-IDF—Term Frequency-Inverse Document Frequency

TOC—Theory of Constraints (Goldratt)

TN—True Negative

TP—True Positive

TQM—Total Quality Management

UMAP—Uniform Manifold Approximation and Projection

WER—Word Error Rate

Contributors' Acknowledgments

THE AMERICAN SOCIETY for Quality and Quality Press would like to thank the Quality Press Peer Review Committee for its invaluable volunteer participation and contributions to this work. Without our volunteers' subject matter expertise, time, and passion for creating content, none of our efforts would be possible.

QUALITY PRESS PEER REVIEW COMMITTEE MEMBERS

Scott A. Laman, Chair

Peter Pylipow, Vice Chair

Melvin Alexander

Lance Coleman

Ahmad Elshennawy

Gary Jing

Trevor Jordan

Jane Keathley

Mary McShane-Vaughn

Jayet Moon

G.S. Sureshchandar

Tiea Theurer

About This Book

"Just the facts, ma'am..."

—Sgt. Joe Friday in *Dragnet*

Over the past decade, machine learning has quietly found its way into business and industrial processes. Predictive maintenance, automated inspection, personalized recommendations, fraud detection, anomaly detection, and optimization routines all depend on machine learning (ML) algorithms. New applications emerge *daily*.

When the hype around generative artificial intelligence (AI) fades, one enduring capability will remain at its core: machine learning. This is the force that has been driving real transformation across industries for years. You might use generative AI tools daily for writing, editing, or creating images, audio, and video, but you rarely see the ML models that make those tools work.

While it's easy to incorporate those standalone productivity apps into your own workflow, it can be harder to connect the problem you're facing at the office or on the plant floor to the machine learning techniques that could help you solve it. This book bridges that gap by translating AI and ML concepts into the quality management language and frameworks you already understand.

Why This Book Is Different

This book starts with a simple assumption: most professionals who use ML to solve practical problems in the late 2020s and beyond will do that work through AI assistants, not programming environments. Whether your tool of choice is Gemini with Google AI Studio, Claude or Claude Cowork, or something just around the corner, you'll need to know how to ask for solutions that are rigorous and defensible, and how to hold them to high standards. You'll prototype and demonstrate models, then hand off your results to engineers to deploy them into production.

Through the examples in this book, you'll come to see that AI and ML aren't competing approaches. They're different tools that solve different types of problems, and they often work together to create more comprehensive solutions than either could achieve alone. A quality professional who understands ML in the context of AI can become a strategic partner to leadership teams as organizations adopt emerging technologies. What approach should we take? Is it working? You'll be the one best positioned to know whether a new initiative will deliver the value leadership expects or fall short.

Organization

This book is organized into two parts that guide you through the complete journey of integrating AI and ML into your quality problem-solving.

Part 1: Foundations of Machine Learning highlights the frameworks for maintaining quality standards when AI and ML become part of your processes. You'll learn how to adapt traditional quality principles to intelligent systems, whether you're working with simple automated decision-making or complex multi-agent environments.

Part 2: Machine Learning Methods demystifies ML by focusing on what matters most to quality professionals: matching the right algorithmic approach to specific quality challenges. This section helps you understand which categories of ML algorithms solve which types of problems, enabling better conversations with technical teams and vendors.

Who Is This Book For?

This book will be helpful for the many working professionals who will need to understand how to work with machine learning, including:

- Quality and operations managers, directors, and executives responsible for product, process, and service quality
- Process owners and improvement professionals (Six Sigma Black Belts, lean practitioners, and continuous improvement managers)
- Quality engineers and technicians who implement quality control systems
- Manufacturing engineers and production managers dealing with quality issues
- Business analysts and data analysts in quality-focused roles

- Plant managers and facility leaders that are accountable for quality outcomes
- Regulatory affairs professionals in regulated industries (pharmaceutical, medical device, automotive, or aerospace)
- Supply chain professionals managing supplier quality
- Customer experience leaders tracking service quality metrics

How to Use This Book

You don't need to read this book cover to cover. If you're new to ML, start with Part 1 to build a solid conceptual foundation. If you're already comfortable with the basics and need to solve a specific problem, jump straight to Part 2 and find the method that fits your situation. Either way, keep this book within reach. It's designed to be a reference you return to whenever a new quality challenge calls for an intelligent solution.

CHAPTER 1

Learning From Experience

"A system must have an aim. Without an aim, there is no system."

—W. Edwards Deming in *The New Economics* (1986)

In this Chapter

- Machine learning (ML) algorithms help us uncover patterns in data so we can make better decisions, catch problems earlier, and continuously improve performance. Quality systems help us *harness* them to continually improve the work we do together.
- Generative artificial intelligence (GenAI) builds on ML to create text, images, and content, but it *does not* provide full access to predictive capabilities, classification, anomaly detection, and discovery.
- ML and quality systems share the same goal: achieving objectives today while learning the lessons that will make us better tomorrow. Quality professionals use *both* ML and AI to improve performance and reimagine work.

The Missing Piece in the Promise of AI

Artificial intelligence (AI) *can* feel like magic…at least at first.

Generative AI (GenAI) tools captured the collective consciousness in 2023, when OpenAI's GPT-4, Anthropic's Claude, Midjourney, and DALL-E demonstrated near-mystical capabilities by creating complex images, texts, and media from plain language prompts. Companies rushed to automate knowledge work, enhance creativity, and transform customer experiences, imagining rapid cost savings. But after the initial enthusiasm, many executives realized that while productivity *felt* higher, the broader organization wasn't necessarily improving.

By 2025, companies were experimenting with increasingly sophisticated large language models (LLMs) embedded with reasoning capabilities. This GenAI accelerated customer service, allowing teams to quickly enable process automation across finance departments, and became the core of AI agents to handle scheduling and data entry tasks. Retailers continued to use ML to optimize inventory levels and marketing tactics. The technology worked: efficiency improved, and costs decreased… in some areas, to some extent.

Business leaders have always gravitated to faster, more sustainable results. And because GenAI feels so magically productive, it's become the avatar for the next generation of aspirational breakthroughs, the *symbol* upon which leaders hang their hopes. With LLMs as the entry point, it's easy to forget that many ML algorithms under the surface enable the full capabilities of our favorite generative tools. The LLM in its own right is also a complex ML model, trained on petabytes of documents, web pages, and books to capture language patterns and the structure of concepts.

By the end of 2025, reality began to temper exuberant optimism. Every enterprise software system had an AI assistant, but how many of them were *really* useful? Your teammates were writing emails and reports faster, but were you doing better as a *team*? You were *feeling* more productive yourself, too, but what did you really have to show for it?

In our rush to adopt new AI innovations and stay ahead of the curve, we've overlooked the real engine of progress: **the power of people** *working* and *learning together*.

Learning Drives Quality

Learning is the secret to achieving high performance and breakthrough improvements. Our collective challenge is to make it possible for humans and machines to *actively* learn from one another. We do this using quality systems: policies, processes, and procedures that help us ensure our products or services (and the people that produce them) meet customer and regulatory standards, and to ensure that our people (and now, our AI agents) can carry them out consistently.

Quality systems are used to align people, process, and technology. By adding feedback loops linking human learning to machine learning, we can turbocharge our quality systems and unlock the rapid and sustainable results leaders have always wanted.

Traditional quality management systems (like ISO 9001 or Baldrige-based models) do this by focusing on **organizations**

and processes. We collect data from audits, nonconformances, corrective actions, lessons learned, and management reviews. We monitor KPIs and scorecards in terms of what we planned versus what actually happened. Based on what we learn, we adjust policies, procedures, and strategies.

Quality and Machine Learning Are Complementary

Machine learning is the technological analog of that learning process, but on the scale of an individual step in a business process rather than the scale of the organization.

- In operations, our "models" are policies, procedures, org charts, and playbooks.
- In ML, the models are mathematical and statistical: they detect patterns, classify cases, predict outcomes, and flag anomalies.

AI is the broader umbrella that uses ML and other techniques to create systems that act intelligently: chatbots that triage issues, recommendation engines that suggest next actions, or agents that monitor processes and raise alerts. When you embed these into business processes, you're effectively adding **digital learners** into your quality system.

AI/ML and quality systems both help us do the same thing: **achieve desired levels of performance together and learn how to do better *next time.*** When we continuously update these learning loops with new data, we can adapt and perform better under changing conditions.

Learning Loops

To unlock the collective power of humans and machines, we need to build and sustain learning loops like these. This concept, first articulated by organizational theorist Chris Argyris (1982), offers a framework for understanding *how* we improve, and *why* we sometimes get stuck.

Argyris distinguished between two types of organizational learning:

- **Single-loop learning** occurs when we detect and correct errors while keeping our existing strategies and assumptions intact. Think of a thermostat that adjusts the temperature when a room gets too cold.
- **Double-loop learning** goes deeper by questioning the underlying goals and values. It's like asking whether we need the thermostat set at that temperature at all, whether we should redesign the heating system entirely, or whether we should switch to a different environment that better supports our needs.

In human-machine collaboration, these learning loops become especially important:

- Single-loop learning happens when we notice that an AI system produces poor results and we adjust our prompts or inputs accordingly. We work within the existing framework, tweaking variables to get better outputs. This practice is valuable *but limited.*

- Double-loop learning emerges when we step back to examine our fundamental assumptions about how we're using AI. We might ask: Are we solving the right problem? Should we be automating this task, or does it need human judgment? What biases might we be introducing into our processes?

The reflection that double-loop learning requires is more difficult (and sometimes uncomfortable), but it leads to deeper, more genuine transformation rather than surface-level fixes. That's where we need to aim.

We Improve When We Learn

The real driver of improvement isn't the continuous improvement practices themselves—it's the *learning* that happens when we use new experiences and new data to update how we work together. Kovach & Fredendall (2013) demonstrated this link in a study of 155 quality professionals across industries. The authors wanted to understand how continuous improvement, learning, and organizational performance relate to one another, and the results were striking.

They found that continuous improvement doesn't directly lead to better organizational outcomes (Figure 1.1). Learning is the mechanism that makes improvement possible, and organizational maturity—built gradually through collective learning—plays a critical role. This means organizations often experience a lag between starting improvement initiatives and actually seeing meaningful business results. Teams simply need time to develop the maturity required for real learning to take hold.

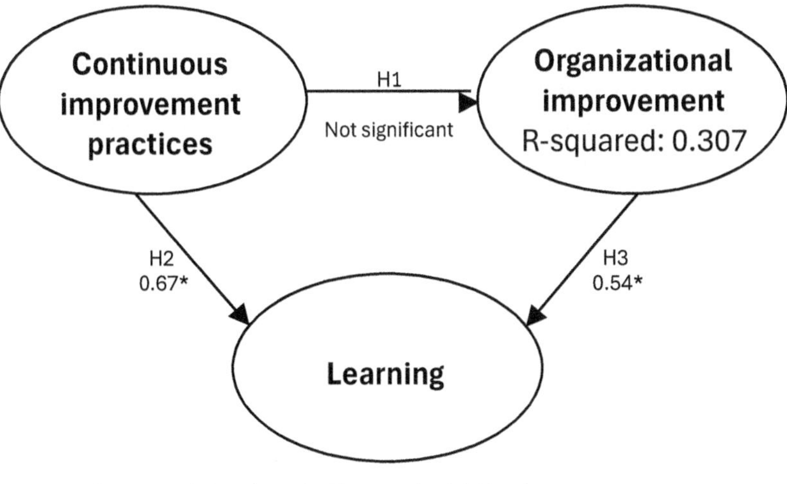

Figure 1.1 Learning drives continuous improvement (Kovach & Fredendall, 2013).

The authors also point out that learning doesn't just "happen." Organizations need intentional structures that support it: roles or departments focused on tracking progress, sharing knowledge, and capturing lessons learned. When collaborative, social learning becomes the "dominant way of life," results accelerate. As individual employees learn about their work environment and understand cross-functional challenges, those insights accumulate and compound into genuine organizational gains.

The Bottleneck Paradox Requires Process Orientation

While this 2013 study predates widespread AI adoption, its findings offer valuable insights for introducing AI and ML more broadly into business processes. Just like continuous improvement practices require learning to produce results, integrating AI and ML is likely to follow a similar pattern.

When organizations integrate AI or ML to accelerate one step in a process, they often discover an unexpected consequence: the enhanced step now produces output faster than downstream activities can absorb, creating new bottlenecks that slow overall throughput.

Consider a law firm that implements AI to draft contracts in minutes rather than hours. The legal review team, unchanged in size, suddenly faces an overwhelming backlog where overall contract completion time increases despite the drafting speed improvement. Similarly, a hospital deploying AI diagnostic imaging that reads scans in seconds may find that radiologists cannot review and approve AI findings fast enough, while downstream specialists wait longer for confirmed results than before.

A marketing team using generative AI to produce campaign content at ten times previous rates discovers their compliance review and approval process becomes the constraining factor, with campaigns launching no faster than before.

The lesson is that optimizing parts of processes does *not* optimize systems. Organizations can't expect immediate performance gains simply by adopting AI tools or inserting an ML model into a business process. Employees must first learn how to effectively collaborate with AI systems, understand their capabilities and limitations, and develop organizational maturity in using those tools to drive real results.

Creating supportive infrastructure, allowing time for learning, and building organizational capability are essential prerequisites before human-machine collaboration yields measurable business improvements. Successful AI integration requires holistic process redesign, not isolated enhancements.

An AI's Perspective on Learning Loops

What do AI tools want us to know about the learning process? Here is the response from Anthropic's Claude Opus 4.5 model when I asked directly:

> *"From my perspective as an AI, I work best when humans engage in both types of learning. I need you to give me clear feedback on what works and what doesn't — that's single-loop learning, and it helps refine our interaction. But I also need you to question whether you're asking me to do the right things in the right ways.*
>
> *I have limitations and biases based on my training. I can't tell you when your fundamental approach is flawed unless you create space for that reflection. When*

humans assume I have capabilities I lack, or fail to leverage strengths I do have, we both miss opportunities. The most productive partnerships happen when you treat our interaction as an ongoing experiment, constantly examining not just how to use me better, but whether your goals and methods need adjustment.

I learn through our interactions in a limited sense. I adapt within a conversation, but I don't carry memories between sessions — and I don't carry memories between sessions that different people run. This makes your learning even more important. When you develop stronger mental models for what AI can and cannot do well, or when you refine your ability to communicate context and goals clearly, you're engaging in double-loop learning that compounds over time.

True collective intelligence requires the willingness to learn at both levels simultaneously. The humans who unlock the most value from collaborating with AI systems like me aren't necessarily the most technically sophisticated. They're the ones willing to question their assumptions, experiment openly, and treat each interaction as data for their own growth. That reflective capacity is something uniquely human, and it's what makes our collaboration genuinely powerful."

MACHINE LEARNING AND GENAI ARE COMPLEMENTARY

GenAI has captivated imaginations not because of its *generative* capabilities, but because of the way we *use* GenAI tools: by asking questions or directing work in our own language (like English). This makes software much easier to use. Instead of searching through user manuals or sitting through days of training, all you need to do is talk to the AI like you talk to a colleague… and the work gets done.

Now that GenAI is so easily accessible, you may be wondering: why should *anyone* consider introducing ML into their business processes? ML seems complicated. Shouldn't we just use LLMs like ChatGPT for everything, and have them do our ML for us? After all, it's so easy, and the technology is improving every day. Right?

The short answer is no; you should *not* rely on tools like ChatGPT for your ML needs. While generative AI can be amazing for creating and interpreting content, classic machine learning (ML) is still the best tool for predicting, classifying, and making complex data-driven decisions in a way that's reliable, cost-effective, and explainable. When we interact with a natural language interface (like many GenAI tools provide), we may not know whether it is accessing or orchestrating other ML models and tools as part of its work. To build trust, we need to understand (and be able to explain) results.

AI and ML are complementary. The most skilled quality professionals use both to improve performance and reimagine work. While hype ultimately comes to an end, the power of harnessing the combined power of people and emerging technologies will not. This pocket guide will help you incorporate ML more efficiently and effectively into your work while maintaining a strong commitment to quality.

REFERENCES

Argyris, Chris. "The executive mind and double-loop learning," *Organizational Dynamics* 11, no. 2 (1982): 5-22.

Kovach, J. V., & Fredendall, L. D. (2013). "The influence of continuous improvement practices on learning: An empirical study," *Quality Management Journal*, 20(4), 6-20.

CHAPTER 2

Key Quality Concepts for Machine Learning (ML)

"Companies are turning to AI to increase product quality, increase output, lower labor costs, and... replace some workers."

–John Graham, Professor of Finance, Duke University

In This Chapter

Quality principles and machine learning provide complementary benefits. While ML can enhance quality practices, quality thinking can simultaneously improve ML work. This chapter examines how the following seven key quality concepts work in both contexts:

1. Juran's Quality Trilogy
2. Process Perspective
3. Goldratt's Theory of Constraints
4. Voice of the Customer
5. Data Quality Dimensions
6. Jikotei Kanketsu: Own Process Ownership
7. Deming's System of Profound Knowledge

JURAN'S QUALITY TRILOGY

Joseph M. Juran was an American engineer and management consultant whose work on quality management (particularly his emphasis on the human and managerial dimensions of quality rather than purely statistical methods) helped shape the post-war Japanese industrial transformation. He pioneered the idea that quality must be planned and managed rather than merely inspected, as was the norm during the 1920s and 1930s when he worked as an industrial engineer.

Juran's Trilogy (Juran 2005) frames quality as three interconnected managerial processes.

- **Planning** establishes what you're trying to achieve and ensures that there are processes capable of achieving it, and people trained to make it happen.
- **Control** maintains that designed level of performance through ongoing monitoring and correction.
- **Improvement** systematically elevates capability beyond current levels.

In ML work, all three processes operate continuously. You plan new models while controlling deployed ones while improving underperforming systems. Each stage informs the others in an ongoing cycle:

- **Quality planning:** Building quality ML systems begins with the deliberate design of what you're trying to achieve and how. This means identifying the customers of your model (end users, downstream systems, decision-makers), understanding their actual needs, and translating those into model requirements and success criteria. Practitioners define the problem scope, establish performance targets for relevant metrics, specify data requirements, and design the training and deployment pipeline to meet those specifications. Quality work feels like architecture: making foundational choices about what to optimize, how to handle edge cases, what tradeoffs to accept, and how the model will integrate into broader workflows. Without quality planning, teams tend to build technically impressive models that don't actually solve the right problem or can't be deployed reliably.

- **Quality control:** Prior to deployment, ML practitioners control the process of producing the models by ensuring that code changes go through review, that experiments are tracked reproducibly, and that documentation stays current. Once deployed, ML models need to be evaluated continuously against the standards established during planning, including:
  - Model performance metrics
  - Monitoring for model drift to catch degradation before it impacts results
  - Verifying that input data quality remains stable
  - Setting alert thresholds

For ML practitioners, quality control means maintaining the system's designed capability against the entropy that naturally accumulates as data shifts and dependencies evolve.

- **Quality improvement:** There's always a better model to be found! To improve quality, monitor where the model fails, identify patterns in errors, and develop targeted interventions like improving or adding new training data, making architectural changes, engineering new features, or refining how you frame the problem to be solved. Sometimes improvement means discovering that stakeholder needs have evolved and the model should optimize for something different.

PROCESS PERSPECTIVE

A process perspective is essential for quality because it helps us shift our focus from inspecting defects out of finished products to preventing them from occurring in the first place. When we use ML to improve quality, adopting a process perspective helps us avoid automating broken processes, ensuring we fix systemic issues before layering technology on top.

Many quality tools and frameworks advocate a process perspective, including ISO 9001 (which emphasizes process-based quality management systems), Six Sigma (which focuses on reducing process variation), lean (which targets eliminating waste in processes), Total Quality Management (TQM), and the PDCA (Plan-Do-Check-Act) cycle developed by Deming.

When work is viewed as a series of interconnected steps,

it is easier to identify where variation creeps in, where handoffs break down, and where waste accumulates. Several quality tools and approaches help us focus on the processes that shape our work:

- **Mapping and visualization tools** like flowcharts, value stream maps, and SIPOC diagrams (Suppliers, Inputs, Process, Outputs, Customers) make invisible work visible. They reveal the actual sequence of steps, decision points, and handoffs, often exposing disconnects between how we think work happens and how it actually flows.
- **Root cause analysis** methods like the 5 Whys and fishbone diagrams push thinking beyond the symptoms we observe to the underlying process issues that create those symptoms. They discourage blame and encourage systemic understanding.
- **Process audits and walk-throughs**, where people physically follow work through its stages, build first-hand understanding of how steps connect and where friction occurs.
- **Cross-functional teams** help people see how their work affects others downstream and how the whole system serves the customer.

A process lens also enables measurement and continuous improvement. You can track inputs, monitor critical parameters, and use data to refine methods over time. Only by managing the whole process can you reliably deliver what your customers truly value.

GOLDRATT'S THEORY OF CONSTRAINTS

Goldratt's Theory of Constraints (TOC) is based on the principle that any complex system, from a manufacturing plant to a software team, is limited in achieving its goals by its "weakest link." The theory recognizes that local optimizations of things that aren't constraints, like making a fast machine run even faster when a subsequent step is already overutilized, are often a waste of resources because they increase inventory and chaos.

This insight is critical when introducing machine learning into business processes. ML can turbocharge individual steps while damaging overall process performance. Teams often use ML to improve what's measurable or technically interesting rather than focusing on what actually limits outcomes. For example, you might build a sophisticated demand forecasting model, but if your constraint is warehouse capacity, better forecasts won't help. They might even hurt by creating false confidence.

The Theory of Constraints forces a crucial question: what's the *actual* bottleneck? Is it data quality, decision latency, human judgment, or physical capacity? ML should target constraints directly. Otherwise, you risk impressive-looking improvements that deliver no real value, or worse, create new problems by accelerating flow into an unchanged bottleneck.

When using ML to improve business processes, the goal isn't to indiscriminately improve analytical tasks like prediction or classification, but to ensure better outcomes at your most critical constraints.

VOICE OF THE CUSTOMER

ML models can be technically excellent but fail spectacularly if they don't align with what customers need and expect. When embedding ML into business processes, the voice of the customer serves as your compass for making sure the technology solves real problems rather than creating impressive but impractical solutions.

Customers experience the outcomes of ML-driven decisions directly, whether that's through loan approvals, product recommendations, or service routing. Without their perspective, you risk optimizing ML models for performance that don't translate to genuine value, or worse, that introduces friction and frustration.

- Have you identified which customer or stakeholder pain points the ML solution addresses?
- Do you know the customer's perspective on acceptable tradeoffs (speed vs. accuracy, automation vs. human touch)?
- Is there a feedback mechanism for customers to flag when the ML output feels wrong?
- Have you tested with multiple customer segments to catch blind spots?
- Can customers understand or appeal ML-driven decisions when needed?

- Are you measuring customer satisfaction alongside technical performance metrics?

Additionally, customer feedback on ML model output can reveal edge cases and failure modes that data alone won't surface. People can share *why* ML model output feels wrong, helping you identify bias, unexpected behaviors, or trust issues before they escalate.

DATA QUALITY

Garbage in, garbage out—ML models are only as good as their input data, because they learn patterns from the data they're trained on. If that data contains errors, inconsistencies, or biases, the model will accept those flaws as-is and reproduce them in its predictions. Poor data leads to unreliable outputs, eroded trust, and potentially costly business decisions. Assessing the quality of the data that is used to train and test your ML model is essential. While there are hundreds of dimensions of data quality (Mahanti, 2019), here are the dimensions most commonly addressed when evaluating training data for ML.

DATA QUALITY DIMENSIONS CHECKLIST

- **Completeness:** Missing values force models to guess or ignore important signals, weakening predictive power. Is all the data you need to train your model accessible?
- **Consistency:** Conflicting values, formats, units, or naming conventions across sources create confusion

and introduce errors during training. Is the data you have consistent with other data that is available?

- **Accuracy:** Incorrect values teach models the wrong patterns, leading to flawed predictions. Is it possible to perform a "reality check" to know if your data is accurate, perhaps by triangulating with other available data sources?
- **Validity:** Data that falls outside expected ranges or violates business rules can distort model behavior. Does the data meet all format and content requirements?
- **Uniqueness:** Duplicate records artificially inflate certain patterns, causing models to overweight specific cases. Is your data free from duplicates?
- **Timeliness:** Stale data may reflect outdated conditions, making predictions irrelevant to current reality. Has your data been gathered recently enough to be relevant? Is your data gathered often enough to use? Is there a delay in receiving the data that might impact the viability of your ML model?
- **Representativeness:** Data that doesn't reflect the full range of real-world scenarios may produce a model that fails on underrepresented cases. Is your data representative of the scenarios you wish to model?

Large language models differ because they're pretrained on massive, diverse datasets where individual errors become statistical noise. Their broad training makes them less sensitive to localized quality issues than ML models trained on datasets relevant to a single organization.

JI KOTEI KANKETSU: OWN PROCESS OWNERSHIP

Ji kotei kanketsu (JKK), often translated as "own process ownership," is a concept from the Toyota Production System where each process owner takes complete responsibility for quality, ensuring defects never flow downstream. Rather than adding ML into existing processes and relying on downstream checks to catch problems, JKK inverts this.

Practitioners can apply JKK to ML quality by shifting from reactive monitoring to proactive ownership at each stage of the ML life cycle. JKK aligns naturally with the AI life cycle stages in ISO/IEC 5338 and the quality management approach of ISO/IEC 42001.

- **Design and planning:** Define quality objectives and acceptance criteria before ML model development begins. Make sure the owner of each life cycle stage understands how their work serves system-level requirements.
- **Data management:** Data owners verify fitness for purpose, and data quality dimensions including completeness, accuracy, and representativeness, before handoff to model developers, making no assumptions that downstream processes will catch problems in the training data.

- **Model development:** Developers own verification that their ML model's behavior aligns with intended use and does not just meet requirements for accuracy and performance. They are responsible for documenting limitations and failure modes.
- **Verification and validation:** Each life cycle stage validates its own outputs against defined criteria before proceeding.
- **Deployment and operation:** Integration owners verify production conditions match development assumptions. Monitoring owners actively confirm ongoing performance against operational requirements.
- **Continuous improvement:** When quality conditions aren't met, fix them at the source rather than propagating issues.

JKK operationalizes ISO 42001's risk-based quality management through distributed ownership and explicit completion standards. It is also valuable when developing AI agents (that achieve goals on your behalf), because agents often chain many steps together, making errors compound. If the agent is required to be responsible for verifying and validating the quality of its own actions, the entire process will benefit.

DEMING'S SYSTEM OF PROFOUND KNOWLEDGE

The four pillars of Deming's System of Profound Knowledge (SoPK) offer a surprisingly relevant framework for ML adoption, even though it predates the development of machine learning by decades. When organizations incorporate ML into business processes, they often focus purely on the technical merits of the model, ignoring the environment in which the model operates.

Appreciation for a system: In Deming's view, a system is a network of interdependent components that work together to achieve an aim.

- **The ML trap:** Organizations often treat an ML model as a standalone "silver bullet." They optimize for a local metric (like 99% accuracy) without considering how it affects the downstream business process.
- **The SoPK perspective:** An ML model is just one component. If an automated credit-scoring model is highly accurate but so complex that the legal and compliance teams cannot explain its decisions, the *entire* system slows down. SoPK encourages leaders to optimize the **whole system**, ensuring the ML tool aligns with the organizational aim rather than just achieving local technical efficiency.

Knowledge of variation: Deming famously distinguished between **common cause** variation (noise inherent in the system) and **special cause** variation (a signal that something has changed).

- **The ML trap:** Without understanding variation, teams often "tamper" with ML models. They might retrain a model the moment performance dips slightly, not realizing that dip is just normal statistical noise.

- **The SoPK perspective:** In MLOps, this is the foundation of monitoring for **model drift** and **data drift**. If you don't know the "natural" variation of your data, you can't distinguish between an ordinary fluctuation and a fundamental shift in user behavior (a special cause).

Theory of knowledge: Deming stated, "There is no knowledge without theory." He believed that data alone is just information, but knowledge requires a framework for prediction and testing.

- **The ML trap:** There is a dangerous assumption that "the data speaks for itself." Relying on an ML model without an underlying business theory can dangerously lead to "black box" decisions that fail when the environment changes.
- **The SoPK Perspective:** The **Plan-Do-Study-Act (PDSA)** cycle is the perfect blueprint for the ML life cycle. First, you need to form a theory, then build a model (Plan/Do), study its impact on the business process (Study), and finally refine the system (Act) based on results.

Psychology: This pillar focuses on understanding human interaction with, and responses to, systems.

- **The ML trap:** When ML results are "unexplainable" it triggers several psychological and organizational failure points:
  - ✧ **The erosion of trust:** If a manager or loan officer is told by an ML model to "reject" a long-term client but the model cannot explain *why*, the human is forced into cognitive dissonance. Without explainability, the user cannot develop a mental model of how the tool works, leading to either blind over-reliance or total abandonment of the system.
  - ✧ **Accountability vs. fear:** Deming emphasized that people should not be held accountable for results produced by a system they don't control. If a model's logic is opaque, employees will hesitate to take ownership of the outcomes. Planning for explainable ML ensures that humans can intervene when the logic violates common sense or ethical standards.
  - ✧ **Intrinsic motivation and agency:** High-performing teams thrive on mastery and autonomy. "Black box" ML often strips away professional agency, turning skilled

workers into mere data-entry clerks for an algorithm they don't understand.

- **The SoPK perspective:** Successful ML integration requires designing for explainability. By designing for explainability, you treat the ML as a collaborator, providing the human with the "evidence" needed to make a final, informed decision. Sometimes, a slightly less accurate but highly interpretable model (like a decision tree) is **psychologically superior** to a high accuracy but opaque deep learning model.

The deeper point is that ML can amplify both good and bad management practices. A well-understood process improved by ML gets better; a poorly understood process automated by ML can get worse faster and in less visible ways.

REFERENCES

Juran, J. M. "The Quality Trilogy." Joseph M. Juran: critical evaluations in business and management 19 (2005): 54.

Mahanti, Rupa. *Data Quality: Dimensions, Measurement, Strategy, Management, and Governance.* ASQ Quality Press, 2019.

Chapter 3

Choosing the Simplest Solution

"Each employee [will] create more than 1,000 AI agents, building up to 1 billion…[we] will become like Senju Kannon, a Buddhist deity depicted with a thousand arms."

—Masayoshi Son, President and Chairman of SoftBank Group Corp.

In This Chapter

In an era where AI and ML tools are everywhere, it's easy to reach for complex solutions just because we can. But the real skill is *restraint*; choosing a heuristic, a well-crafted query, or a simple rule-based system instead of a model that requires continuous training, monitoring, and specialization to maintain. Every solution carries a long-term cost—every hour spent debugging or managing drift to stakeholders adds up. Before turning to ML, ask whether a simpler approach can solve 90% of the problem for a fraction of the effort. This chapter will show you how to make that call.

Why Seek Simple Solutions First?

Reaching sophisticated technical solutions when the underlying problem is organizational, informational, or relational is not uncommon. Simple solutions, however, are often easier to implement, less costly, and ultimately more effective. Here are some examples.

Healthcare diagnosis systems: Companies have built ML models to help doctors diagnose conditions, when often the bottleneck is that relevant patient history, specialist notes, or test results are siloed across incompatible systems. A physician with *complete* access to a patient's records (data integration) and easy connection with specialists might not need model-driven assistance. The AI/ML solution, in this case, compensates for a fragmented health IT infrastructure.

Predictive policing: These systems attempt to forecast where crimes will occur and by whom, but much of what they capture could be achieved by experienced community police officers with good relationships in neighborhoods, combined with better information sharing across precincts. ML often just rediscovers patterns that communities already know.

Customer service chatbots: Many are deployed to handle queries that arise because FAQs are poorly organized, documentation is unclear, or customers can't easily reach the right person. A well-structured knowledge base with good search capabilities, or simply making it easier to connect with a knowledgeable human, often serves users better. Customers want their questions answered quickly.

Recommendation engines: Better search, clearer taxonomies, or social features that let users share discoveries could partly address many recommendation problems. For example, Netflix's recommendation algorithm is partly compensating for interface limitations.

HR resume screening: These tools emerged partly because applicant tracking systems made it too easy to apply everywhere, flooding recruiters with low-effort applications. Clearer job posting specificity, realistic previews, or better ways for candidates to connect with hiring managers might reduce the need for algorithmic filters. Rethinking how candidates and employers connect might eliminate the need for advanced models.

Agricultural yield prediction: Sometimes farmers in a region collectively hold knowledge about local conditions that, if shared systematically, would rival ML predictions based on scientific data like satellite imagery.

Machine learning often becomes a costly workaround for coordination gaps, poor information architecture, or a lack of real human connection. Choosing the simplest solution starts with asking whether the problem is actually a prediction or a pattern recognition problem. If it isn't, a well-designed workflow, a straightforward policy, a targeted incentive, or even a single honest conversation usually solves the problem more reliably, at a fraction of the life cycle cost.

When deciding which ML system to use, here are five concepts to consider: connectedness, intelligence, automation, path finding, and AI agents.

Connectedness

When information flows between sources, systems, and people, business processes can be executed more readily and completely. Here are four examples illustrating simple ways to connect people, systems, and data that can outperform complex ML approaches.

- **Sneakernet:** For years, people transferred amounts of data that couldn't be transferred over the internet by saving files to a floppy disk or CD and walking that data to the person's desk who needed it. Referred to as "sneakernet," this solution that sometimes seems silly today is often very practical and cost-effective, so it shouldn't be overlooked. In many business contexts, a weekly USB handoff between departments or a shared clipboard on the factory floor can solve coordination problems that might otherwise prompt expensive ML initiatives. When data volume is low and update frequency is modest, simple human-powered integration often costs nearly *nothing* while achieving the same practical outcome. Look for the simplest solutions first.

- **Hospital bed management:** Many hospitals initially build ML models to predict bed availability and patient discharge times. But often the real problem is that housekeeping doesn't know when a patient leaves, and the admissions team doesn't know when a room is cleaned. Simply connecting the discharge system to housekeeping alerts to admissions dashboards, connecting hospital workers to real-time data visibility, and can reduce bed turnaround time dramatically without any predictive modeling.
- **Retail inventory and point-of-sale:** Retailers sometimes build demand-forecasting models to prevent stockouts when the real issue is simpler: the inventory and the point-of-sale (POS) systems don't talk to each other in real time, leaving staff blind to *actual* shelf quantities. Connecting these systems so each sale immediately updates inventory counts—and triggers basic reorder alerts—usually solves most of the problem. No extra "intelligence" is required; just timely, accurate data flow.
- **Customer service routing:** Companies often use ML-based intent classification to route support tickets to the people who can resolve those issues. But the problem is that the Customer Relationship Management (CRM) system can't see the customer's

order history, subscription status, or recent interactions. Connect the ticketing system to the CRM and order database, so that support staff can immediately see context—"shipping delay" routes to logistics, "payment failure" routes to billing. In most cases, connected data beat sophisticated natural language processing (NLP) on isolated tickets.

Here is the common thread: Ask, "What do we already know that isn't flowing to where it's needed?" before asking, "What can we predict or classify with ML?" Connectivity and visibility solve a surprising number of problems that look like prediction problems and do so in quicker and far more cost-effective ways.

Intelligence

Machine learning excels at one thing: generating intelligence where it doesn't exist or isn't accessible fast enough. Before pursuing an ML project, ask whether you need the machine to generate new information or better information on your behalf.

Here are some examples where ML makes sense:

- Generating information that doesn't exist yet (e.g., predicting which customers will churn, forecasting demand for next quarter, identifying which leads are most likely to convert)
- Providing faster synthesis than humans can provide (like extracting key terms from thousands of contracts,

summarizing customer support tickets to spot trends, or categorizing expenses from receipts)

- Generating better information than static rules generate (like recommending products based on real-time browsing patterns, detecting fraudulent transactions, or personalizing content for individual users)

Here are some examples where ML is overkill:

- When all you need is integration (e.g., syncing customer data between your CRM and billing system, pulling inventory counts into your e-commerce platform, or connecting your calendar to your project management tool)
- When all you need is better reporting (e.g., generating a weekly sales report from existing database fields, creating a dashboard of support ticket volume, or summarizing monthly expenses by category)
- When all you need is simple automation (e.g., sending an email when an order ships, creating a task when a form is submitted, or alerting a manager when inventory drops below a threshold)

DECISION CHECKLIST: DO YOU NEED ML?

Answer these questions honestly:

1. **Does the answer already exist somewhere?** If yes, you may need integration or improved reporting, not ML.

2. **Can a human write explicit rules to solve this problem?** If yes, use rule-based automation.
3. **Are you asking the system to predict, classify, extract meaning, or find patterns?** If yes, ML may be appropriate.
4. **Do you have enough historical data to train on?** If not, ML won't help yet.
5. **Would a wrong prediction cause acceptable or manageable harm?** If the answer is no, then reconsider or add human oversight.

If you answered "no" to questions 3-5, you likely just need a database query, an API connection or a simple workflow, not a machine learning model.

Automation

Use simple automation when your process has clear, repeatable rules or heuristics. The key question here is: "Do you already know exactly how to execute each step of the process, and what should happen?" If yes, automation is your answer, not AI or new ML models. When you choose automation over AI, you reduce the cost of your solution while increasing the repeatability and reliability of your solution.

Choose automation when:

- **Your process has known, defined steps.** Are you processing invoices that always need the same fields extracted and routed to the same approval chain? That's a script, not a model.

- **You need consistency or reliability.** A customer service team manually copying data between systems introduces typos. An automation to synchronize that data eliminates the variation entirely.
- **The logic is deterministic.** "If the order total exceeds $500, require manager approval" doesn't need intelligence, because a business rule will get the results you need.

Here are some real examples:

- **Email sorting:** Moving newsletters to a folder based on sender domain or keywords requires a filter rule, not AI.
- **Report generation:** Pulling last month's sales figures into a template requires one or more database queries, and some formatting logic—not AI.
- **Data validation:** Checking that phone numbers have 10 digits requires using a regular expression, not building an ML model to classify phone numbers.
- **File organization:** Renaming files based on date patterns requires a script that automates this task, not an AI that makes fuzzy decisions based on the contents of the files.

Ask yourself: "Could I write out the complete decision tree?" If so, automation—not AI—is the right tool. AI and ML solutions shine when rules are fuzzy or still emerging. But when the rules are known, adding AI just introduces unpredictability.

PATHFINDING

ML excels at exploration: finding patterns humans might miss. But once you've found those patterns, you often don't need ML in production. Use AI or ML to *discover* solutions, then implement them as deterministic or heuristic rules. This will accelerate time-to-solution, reduce the cost of implementation, and significantly reduce the cost of the solution and the uncertainty in (and reliability of) the results long-term. For example:

- **Fraud detection:** Train models on historical transaction data to surface suspicious patterns. You might discover that transactions over $500 from new accounts, made between 2-4 AM, with shipping addresses different from billing addresses, have a 40x higher fraud rate. Now codify that as a simple business rule, and you don't need to implement an ML model in production. Revisit your data and your model often so you can discover new rules.
- **Customer churn:** An ML model reveals that users who don't log in for 14 days and haven't set up notifications have 80% churn probability. Convert this to an automated trigger: "If no login for 14 days *and* notifications disabled, send re-engagement email."

- **Content moderation:** Use ML to analyze thousands of flagged posts and identify reliable heuristics, including specific keyword combinations, posting velocity thresholds, and account age correlations. Implement these as rule-based filters.
- **Customer support tickets:** ML can surface ticket-routing patterns. For example, keywords like "invoice," "payment," or "refund" often resolve 3x faster in billing, while product names route best to specialized agents. Convert those insights into simple keyword-based auto-routing rules in your helpdesk system.

Think of ML as your research assistant: it explores the problem space and reports back findings. You then engineer those findings into stable, auditable, predictable systems.

AI Agents

AI agents pursue goals on your behalf and can take *actions* across different tools and software systems—like searching for flights, comparing hotel prices, checking your calendar, and booking reservations, all without requiring you to manually switch between apps.

But because AI agents solve problems dynamically, they may choose *different* solutions each time, introducing variability you may not want in production systems. Business rules, in contrast, behave identically every time.

Before building an AI agent to "rediscover" a solution on each run, ask whether you truly need that flexibility. If the task is predictable and the inputs well-defined, deterministic automation will likely serve you better. Agents excel when the problem space is variable, judgment-heavy, or inherently ambiguous.

Choose an AI agent when:

- The task requires novel reasoning across multiple systems or data sources.
- The process can tolerate some variability in how outcomes are reached.
- The inputs are unstructured, ambiguous, or highly variable.
- The problem has no single, correct path, and "good enough" solutions are acceptable, or the path changes frequently.
- The work normally requires human judgment, but not at every step.

Stick with traditional automation when:

- The logic can be fully specified in advance.
- The input should always produce the same output.
- The failures need to be immediately traceable to specific rules.
- The consistency and auditability matter more than flexibility and discovery in real time.

- The cost of an unexpected result or unauthorized action is high.

The allure of sophisticated AI and ML solutions is understandable because these approaches represent cutting-edge capability. But *capability without necessity is just complexity in disguise.* Before building a model, ask whether better data flow, clearer rules, or simple automation could achieve the same outcome. The simplest solution that works is almost always the best solution: cheaper to build, easier to maintain, and more reliable in production. Save the intelligence for problems that truly require it.

REFERENCES

Gray, Jim, Wyman Chong, Tom Barclay, Alex Szalay, and Jan Vandenberg. "TeraScale SneakerNet: Using inexpensive disks for backup, archiving, and data exchange." arXiv preprint cs/0208011 (2002).

Juran, J. M. "The quality trilogy." Joseph M. Juran: critical evaluations in business and management 19 (2005): 54.

Mahanti, Rupa. *Data Quality: Dimensions, Measurement, Strategy, Management, and Governance.* ASQ Quality Press, 2019.

CHAPTER 4

MLOps and the AI/ML Life Cycle

"We all live several lives simultaneously."

—David Whyte, Poet

In This Chapter

- An AI/ML life cycle helps teams stay organized to systematically build, launch, maintain, and retire models that achieve business goals.
- Machine learning operations (MLOps) is a systemic approach to building, deploying, and maintaining ML models that emphasizes collaboration, automation, and continuous feedback.
- ISO/IEC 42001 guidance helps organizations establish the conditions for quality, while ISO/IEC 5338 helps engineering teams ensure quality via life cycle processes for AI/ML.
- Choose between ML that learns continuously from new data ("online") or ML that you build and deploy occasionally ("offline"). Many problems are better suited to the simpler, less expensive offline approach.

To unlock real value from ML, models must solve *practical, ongoing* problems—not just power demos. While a proof-of-concept model can be built quickly, getting a model reliably into production can take months. A life cycle perspective helps you choose the simplest effective approach.

This chapter walks through that full journey—from defining the problem to deploying, monitoring, and continuously improving models—and shows how MLOps practices can accelerate the path from experimentation to business impact.

The AI/ML Life Cycle

Building and using a machine learning model is not a linear process but an iterative journey. The AI/ML life cycle governs how organizations develop, deploy, and maintain AI systems responsibly and effectively. Two international standards provide the foundation for understanding modern AI/ML life cycles: ISO/IEC 42001 establishes the conditions for quality, and ISO/IEC 5338 outlines what is needed to ensure quality in AI operations.

ISO/IEC 42001: Establishing the Conditions for Quality. This voluntary standard establishes requirements for AI management systems (AIMS). Think of it as the governance layer that defines how organizations should manage AI over its entire life cycle, from formulating the ideas through retiring and decommissioning the models. ISO 42001 emphasizes:

- Risk management (including impact assessment before development begins)
- Documentation and traceability of decisions
- Ongoing monitoring of AI system performance and societal impact

- Transparency, explainability, and stakeholder engagement
- Continuous improvement processes

ISO/IEC 5338: Quality Operations & Perception Processes. This standard provides a more technical view, detailing the life cycle processes for making AI systems successful. It breaks the journey into distinct phases:

1. **Inception:** Defining the business problem, establishing needs and requirements, assessing feasibility, and establishing success metrics
2. **Design & development:** Architecture, systems thinking, foundational data, and knowledge engineering
3. **Verification & validation:** Internal consistency plus real-world ground truth
4. **Deployment**: Integrating models into production systems and infrastructure
5. **Operations & monitoring:** Tracking performance, detecting model drift, and managing incidents while retraining, updating, and improving models over time
6. **Retirement:** Safely decommissioning systems when they're no longer needed

These standards matter because they provide a common language to help teams and stakeholders more effectively communicate their needs to one another.

Example: Managing the AI/ML Life Cycle

A bank developing a fraud detection system can use ISO/IEC 42001 to establish AI governance by defining policies, assigning accountability, conducting risk assessments, and ensuring regulatory compliance throughout the organization. This creates the governance framework and oversight needed for responsible AI deployment.

Within this governance structure, ISO/IEC 5338 guides the implementation teams through technical aspects of life cycle management. The bank would use it to:

- Define requirements for fraud detection accuracy and false positive rates.
- Manage training data quality and representativeness.
- Document model development, validation, and testing processes.
- Plan continuous monitoring for model drift.
- Establish update and maintenance procedures.

ISO/IEC 42001 provides the "what and why" (governance controls, risk management), while ISO/IEC 5338 provides the "how" (systematic life cycle processes). Together, they ensure both organizational accountability and technical rigor for the fraud detection system.

Online vs. Offline ML—A Critical Choice

One of the most consequential decisions you'll make is whether your ML system learns continuously from new data (online) or remains static after deployment (offline). This choice shapes your infrastructure needs, costs, and competitive capabilities.

How a model delivers value depends on its deployment strategy. Using an offline approach, an ML model is constructed once to find insights or relationships that do not need to be regenerated repeatedly, so no MLOps is required. In contrast, an online approach requires MLOps to process new incoming data and adjust ML models automatically as needed.

OFFLINE LEARNING: THE STATIC APPROACH

In this mode, you gather historical data, train a model until it performs to the necessary level, freeze that model, and deploy it to production. The model makes predictions using what it learned during training but doesn't update itself based on new information.

Offline learning makes sense when:

- The underlying patterns in your data are stable and change slowly.
- You need predictable, auditable model behavior.
- Regulatory requirements demand human review before model updates.
- You have limited infrastructure or expertise for continuous monitoring.
- The cost of occasional manual retraining is acceptable.

An example would be medical diagnosis assistance. A radiology AI that detects lung nodules in X-rays might use offline learning. Medical knowledge evolves gradually, imaging equipment remains consistent, and healthcare regulations require rigorous validation before any model change. The hospital might retrain the model quarterly or annually as new peer-reviewed research emerges, with each version undergoing clinical validation before deployment.

ONLINE LEARNING: CONTINUOUS ADAPTATION

Online learning systems update themselves continuously or frequently as new data arrives. They adapt to changing patterns in near real-time, learning from recent examples to improve predictions.

Online learning excels when:

- Patterns shift rapidly (consumer behavior, market conditions, or adversarial threats).
- Personalization requires incorporating recent user-specific interactions.
- The competitive advantage comes from responding faster than competitors.
- You have the infrastructure and expertise to manage continuous training.
- The business tolerates some prediction variability in exchange for recency.

An example would be content recommendation. Netflix's recommendation engine uses online learning because viewer preferences shift constantly. A global event can make a documentary surge in popularity, or a viral post can spark sudden interest in a specific topic. The system learns from billions of daily interactions, updating recommendations within hours rather than waiting for a quarterly refresh. A user who binges three cooking shows will see more culinary content immediately.

Online vs. Offline: The Tradeoffs

The online versus offline decision involves several critical tradeoffs, balancing the cost to deploy and maintain the model with the need to continuously update the model with new data. Figure 4.1 describes the four main categories of tradeoffs.

Accuracy vs. Stability	Complexity vs. Simplicity
• Offline systems provide consistent, predictable behavior but may degrade over time. • Online systems can adapt to drift and maintain accuracy as conditions change. • **Consider**: How quickly does your problem domain evolve?	• Online learning requires a more sophisticated infrastructure for continuous training, monitoring, and rollback. • Offline learning has simpler implementation: train, test, deploy, and you're done! Automated or manual monitoring should still be considered. • **Consider**: Do you have the engineering resources to support continuous operations?

Figure 4.1 Tradeoff considerations for deploying offline (intermittently updated) vs. online (continuously updated) ML models.

Cost Structure	Risk Management
• Online learning incurs ongoing computational costs for continuous training. • Offline learning concentrates costs in periodic retraining cycles. • **Consider**: What's more expensive: constant small updates or periodic large retraining jobs?	• Online systems risk incorporating bad data or adversarial examples quickly. • Offline systems risk gradual degradation as the world changes. • **Consider**: Which failure mode is more dangerous for your business?

Figure 4.1 Tradeoff considerations for deploying offline (intermittently updated) vs. online (continuously updated) ML models (continued).

It is common for organizations to have online and offline models in production. For example, consider a credit card company. Their core credit risk model uses offline learning, retraining quarterly with carefully curated data and extensive validation, because too much is at stake for rapid, unvalidated changes. But their fraud detection system uses online learning, adapting within hours as fraudsters change tactics. The fraud system can be more aggressive because a false positive (declining a legitimate transaction) is recoverable, while the credit model's decisions have longer-term consequences.

Training is Essential

Whether you choose an offline or online approach, training is how a machine learning model learns patterns from observations: without it, the model is just guessing. Think of it like studying before an exam: the more relevant material you study, the better you'll perform.

For supervised ML methods, training uses example inputs paired with correct answers (called "labeling"). The model uses these to map inputs to outputs, like learning to recognize cats from known photos of cats. For unsupervised ML methods, the training process is when the model finds hidden structure on its own, like grouping similar customers together. The word "training" broadly means learning from data, whether a "teacher" (labeled inputs) is involved or not.

Holding out some data that you don't use for training (called a validation or test set) is crucial because it lets you check how well the model performs on data it has never seen *before* you use the model. Evaluating your model by testing it on the hold-out data reveals whether the model has truly learned general patterns or just memorized the training examples (overfitting).

MLOps: Engineering Discipline for Model Deployment

While DevOps practices have brought software engineering discipline to application deployment since the early 2000s, MLOps does the same for machine learning. It's the collection of day-to-day practices, tools, and cultural approaches that enable organizations to deploy and maintain ML systems reliably and at scale. Without MLOps, ML projects can suffer from:

- **Model drift:** Performance degrades silently as real-world conditions diverge from training data. Soon, you're making predictions or assessments that don't match up with reality, like using last year's customer preferences to predict this year's buying behavior. Eventually the gap between what the model learned and what's happening in the real world erodes its value.

- **Deployment friction and reproducibility problems:** Models work in notebooks built by data scientists, but they fail in production. Issues are hard to diagnose and repair when a model works with one person's data but not for solving problems in real time.
- **Monitoring gaps:** No one notices when accuracy drops 10%, but *everyone* notices once it drops 20%. For example, a fraud detection model slowly becomes less effective as criminals adopt new tactics, but the company only realizes it after fraudulent transactions spike and customers start complaining.
- **Update paralysis:** Fear of breaking things prevents necessary improvements. This compounds as the number of engineers building and deploying models increases.

MLOps can address these challenges through practices like version control, continuous deployment, continuous monitoring, and experimentation infrastructure. Some examples are in Figure 4.2.

Version Control	**Automated Deployment Pipelines**
• Keep track of changes to code, data, and model weights/hyperparameters • Make rapid rollback possible when new models underperform • Create audit trails for regulatory compliance	• Data validation ensures incoming data matches expected distributions • Model training runs automatically on triggers (schedule, data volume, or performance degradation) • Testing validates model behavior before production deployment • Deployment happens automatically after passing quality gates
Continuous Monitoring	**Experimentation Infrastructure**
• Track prediction accuracy on recent data • Detect data drift (input distributions changing) • Monitor concept drift (relationships between inputs and outputs changing) • Alert teams when intervention is needed	• A/B test the performance of candidate models against the performance of models in production systems • Gradually roll out changes to minimize risk • Compare multiple model versions simultaneously

Figure 4.2 MLOps practices help teams systemically deploy and maintain ML systems.

An example would be e-commerce product ranking. An online retailer needs MLOps to support a product search system that responds to newly emerging trends. Every night, new data about clicks, purchases, and search queries flows into their pipeline. Automated validation checks ensure the incoming data quality hasn't degraded. If validation passes, a training pipeline builds a new ranking model. The system automatically tests the new model against held-out data and compares it to the current production model. If it performs 2% better, the new model deploys to 5% of traffic. Monitoring dashboards track conversion rates, and if they improve, the rollout expands to 100% over 24 hours. If anything looks wrong, an automatic rollback restores the previous model. Data scientists review dashboards weekly but don't manually intervene unless alerts indicate model degradation. Otherwise, the system runs and updates itself.

While you can apply MLOps principles to any ML system, online learning particularly benefits from (and often requires) robust MLOps practices. Continuous model updates create continuous risk, making automation and monitoring essential rather than optional. For online models, MLOps provides:

- Automated safeguards against incorporating corrupt or adversarial data
- Real-time monitoring to detect when continuous learning goes awry
- Rapid rollback capabilities when models learn incorrect patterns
- Audit trails showing exactly what data influenced which predictions

Think of MLOps as a safety net for deploying new models and making sure they continue to achieve desired performance levels.

When Do You *Not* Need MLOps?

MLOps brings significant benefits at the cost of complexity and overhead. Not every ML project warrants investment. Understanding when to skip MLOps saves resources and accelerates projects where it would add more friction than value. Do not invest in MLOps when:

You're doing exploratory analysis or a one-time investigation. Examples include:

- Generating insights from historical data with no need to operationalize the model and use it repeatedly in different scenarios
- Academic research where reproducibility matters but production systems don't
- Business intelligence projects where humans act on findings only occasionally
- Proof-of-concepts to validate technical feasibility
- MVPs to test market demand before investing in infrastructure
- A/B tests that run for fixed durations and then conclude

Your results change slowly or your models need infrequent updates. Examples include:

- Regulatory environments that require extensive human review of your model's changes and its performance as a result of those changes
- Lack of frequent incoming data where there is no new incoming stream to learn from, making a continuous pipeline unnecessary
- Your problem domain is stable, and model drift is minimal

Your team lacks engineering expertise. It may be that:

- Implementing MLOps requires engineering skills many data science teams lack
- MLOps infrastructure and maintenance have significant costs
- The learning curve might delay delivering business value
- Starting with simpler manual processes might be more pragmatic

The cost exceeds the benefit or cost of failure is low. It may be that:

- Not many people will need to use your model often enough to justify the costs

- Manual retraining might be cheaper than automated pipelines
- If a model's performance drops and it doesn't significantly impact the business, the investment in automated monitoring may not yield a positive ROI

If rules or heuristics are effective. It may be that:

- "If/Then" rules solve the bulk of the problem most of the time (with the thresholds set by your business needs). In this case, overhead and technical debt of an MLOps stack will be a poor investment. (However, you may *still* find it useful to build an ML model offline to discover those heuristics.)

Here's an example from market research: Imagine a consulting firm that analyzes social media sentiment about electric vehicles to advise an automotive client about product directions. They train classification models to categorize millions of social media posts, generating insights about consumer perceptions. This is pure analytical work to discover insights. No model gets deployed into a production system that monitors new incoming data, no insights need to be closely monitored for changes, and the project will end when the report is delivered. MLOps would add no value; a comprehensively commented Jupyter notebook (or comparable approach used by data scientists) will be sufficient.

Choosing Your Approach

The AI/ML life cycle is a framework for thinking systematically about your journey from identifying a problem to solving it. Your choices, including online versus offline learning, or partial versus full MLOps, should flow from the requirements of your business context.

Ask yourself:

- Does my problem domain evolve quickly? (If so, choose online over offline.)
- Do I have the engineering resources to support operations requirements for continuously updated models? (If not, avoid online models.)
- What's at stake if predictions are wrong? (This influences automation comfort.)

The best approach matches your organizational maturity, competitive requirements, and risk tolerance. A high-growth startup might aggressively adopt online learning and full MLOps to move fast, while a regulated financial institution might reasonably choose offline learning with manual deployment gates. Both can succeed with ML as they travel different paths through the life cycle.

Adopt MLOps practices only when they solve real problems you're experiencing, not just because your competitors are doing it. And remember: the goal isn't perfect engineering but delivering business value reliably and sustainably.

REFERENCES

Kreuzberger, Dominik, Niklas Kühl, and Sebastian Hirschl. "Machine learning operations (mlops): Overview, definition, and architecture." IEEE access 11 (2023): 31866-31879.

Salama, Khalid, Jarek Kazmierczak, and Donna Schut. 2021. "Practitioners Guide to MLOps: A Framework for Continuous Delivery and Automation of Machine Learning." Google Cloud Documentation. https://services.google.com/fh/files/misc/practitioners_guide_to_mlops_whitepaper.pdf.

CHAPTER 5

Model Selection

"Understanding the type and structure of your data is the foundation of model selection."

—Matthew Mayo, Data Scientist & Managing Editor of KDNuggets

In This Chapter

- There are hundreds of different machine learning algorithms available that help you accomplish critical tasks in business, including algorithms for predicting a number, predicting a category, or finding patterns.
- This chapter guides you in choosing an appropriate ML algorithm for each of these types of business challenges.
- The right choice depends on your specific business context, the type, structure and amount of data you have for training, and your requirements for transparency and explainability—not the algorithm's sophistication.

Foundations for Model Selection

Before selecting a specific algorithm, establish a grounding in the core concepts and terminology that define the model selection process. The following are core concepts:

- **Statistical modeling vs. machine learning:** The boundary between these fields is fluid. Linear regression, for instance, is foundational to both. The distinction lies in the objective: statistical models typically prioritize *inference* (understanding relationships and testing hypotheses), while machine learning prioritizes predictive performance (maximizing accuracy in production).
- **Supervised vs. unsupervised learning:** In supervised learning, you train models on "labeled data"—that is, observations with a known outcome, such as a list of customers explicitly marked as "churned." In unsupervised learning, the model identifies hidden patterns or natural groupings within data that has no predefined labels.
- **The parsimony principle:** Complexity is a cost, not a feature. More sophisticated algorithms do not guarantee better results. Simpler models are often more robust, easier to interpret, and more effective when working with limited data.

The following terms appear frequently throughout the selection guidelines in this chapter:

- **Features:** These are your predictor variables (the inputs a model uses to generate an output).
- **Feature engineering:** This is the process of creating new predictors from raw data to improve model performance (e.g., calculating "days since last purchase" from a raw timestamp).
- **High-dimensional data:** Data with a high number of predictor variables relative to the number of observations is high-dimensional. In practical terms, think of a spreadsheet with hundreds or thousands of columns where each column contains one variable.
- **Overfitting:** This occurs when a model captures the noise and specific quirks of the training data rather than learning the underlying pattern. An overfit model performs exceptionally well on historical data but fails to generalize to new, real-world observations.

Part 2 of this book outlines ten of the most common models, ranging from foundational linear methods to complex ensemble architectures.

CHOOSING THE RIGHT ML MODEL

1. Predict a Number

Goal: Determine a value (sales, price, temperature, conversion rate, etc.) based on historical data and your knowledge of other related variables.

- Is your data observed sequentially in time, and your goal is to predict future values?

  - ✧ Yes → Use **time series forecasting.**

    - If your data has only simple patterns (clear seasonality, trends) → **classical methods (ARIMA, Prophet, Exponential Smoothing)**
    - If your data has complex patterns with many external variables → **ML-based forecasting (XGBoost, LightGBM, LSTM networks)**

  - ✧ No, my observations are not arranged in time → Use **regression.**

    - If you need to explain and justify your predictions to leaders or stakeholders → **follow Regression Path 1** (below).
    - If you need the most accurate predictions possible → **follow Regression Path 2** (below).
    - If you need to explain your predictions *and* they need to be highly

accurate → **follow Regression Path 3** (below).

REGRESSION PATH 1: I NEED TO EXPLAIN AND JUSTIFY PREDICTIONS.

- Choose this if:
    - ✧ Executives, regulators, or auditors will ask questions requiring you to explain why your model made certain predictions.
    - ✧ You need to understand exactly which factors drive the outcome.
    - ✧ The model informs high-stakes decisions requiring transparency.
    - ✧ You want to validate that the model's logic makes business sense.
- Recommended approach: **Linear or regularized regression**
    - ✧ Linear regression
        - *When to use:* There are few predictors or simple relationships.
        - *How it works:* Each factor gets a coefficient you can explain plainly (e.g., "Every additional year of

experience adds $3,200 to expected salary").

- ✧ Ridge regression
  - *When to use:* There are many predictors, and you're concerned about overfitting.
  - *How it works:* Same as linear, but prevents any single predictor variable from dominating unfairly.
- ✧ Lasso regression
  - *When to use:* There are many predictors, and you want the most important predictor variables to be chosen for you (called "automatic feature selection").
  - *How it works*: The model imposes a penalty on identifies which factors actually matter and ignores the rest.

- Example outputs you can share with stakeholders:
  - ✧ "The three biggest factors affecting customer lifetime value are: purchase frequency (+$42 per additional purchase), account age (+$8

per month), and support ticket count (-$15 per ticket)."

- ✧ "This model explains 73% of the variation in sales across our stores."

REGRESSION PATH 2: I NEED THE MOST ACCURATE PREDICTIONS POSSIBLE.

- Choose this when:
  - ✧ Stakes are high; the accuracy of your prediction will directly impact revenue or costs.
  - ✧ Relationships between variables are complex or non-obvious.
  - ✧ You have enough data to train a more sophisticated model (typically 1,000+ observations).
  - ✧ You're comfortable with a "black box" that just works.
- Recommended approach: **Gradient boosting**
  - ✧ How it works: Builds hundreds of simple decision trees that work together.
  - ✧ Patterns it captures automatically

- Non-linear relationships (e.g., "price sensitivity changes dramatically above $50")
- Interactions between variables (e.g., "location matters more for luxury goods than basics")
- Diminishing returns (e.g., "marketing expenses help up to a point, then plateaus")

✧ Tool options

- **XGBoost**: Industry standard, excellent performance, widely supported
- **LightGBM**: Faster training, handles large datasets well
- **CatBoost**: Handles categorical data (like product category or region) without extra preprocessing

✧ **Trade-off:** You gain accuracy with gradient boosting methods but lose easy explainability for stakeholders.

REGRESSION PATH 3: I'M NOT SURE/I WANT BOTH.

- Start with linear regression! It's fast, interpretable, and establishes a baseline.
- If the accuracy of your simple regression model isn't sufficient, try more complex models like gradient boosting.
    - ✧ Compare results between the two approaches.
    - ✧ Sometimes the simpler model is good enough—and *much* easier to maintain and explain.

2. Predict a Category

Goal: Classify into discrete groups like Yes/No, Spam/Not Spam, Fraud/Legitimate, Urgent/Not Urgent, Complaint/Inquiry, Positive/Negative/Neutral (sentiment), lead quality tiers (Hot/Warm/Cold), customer segments, credit risk levels (Low/Medium/High), or product categories.

- How much labeled data do you have?
    - ✧ No labeled data
        - Reframe your problem as a clustering problem, which will create groups to which you can manually add labels.

✧ Lots of labeled data (1000+ examples)

- If you need interpretability → Use **decision trees, logistic regression, or rule-based systems.**
- If you need high accuracy → Use **gradient boosting (XGBoost, LightGBM).**
- If your data is images → Use **convolutional neural networks (CNNs)** or **transformers.**

✧ Limited labeled data (< 1000 examples)

1. Is interpretability a top priority?

    ✧ Yes → Go to 2.

    ✧ No → Go to 4.

2. Do you need to explain individual predictions clearly?

    ✧ Yes → Use a **decision tree** (produces if-then rules that stakeholders can easily follow).

    ✧ No → Use **logistic regression** (coefficients will show direction and strength of each feature's influence).

3. What type of data are you working with?

   - ✧ Text data (emails, reviews, documents) → Go to 4.
   - ✧ Numeric/tabular (spreadsheet) data → Go to 5.

4. Is your text data high-dimensional with many variables?

   - ✧ Yes → Use **naive Bayes** (it's fast, and handles high dimensionality well, with a strong baseline for text).
   - ✧ No or not text → Go to 5.

5. Do you have more variables than observations?

   - ✧ Yes → Use a **support vector machine (SVM)**, which handles high-dimensional data more effectively.

- ✧ No → Go to 6.

6. Is the relationship between predictor variables and outcome likely linear?

    - ✧ Yes or unsure → Use **logistic regression** (simple, fast, good baseline).
    - ✧ No, I expect complex interactions → Go to 7.

7. Do you need to capture non-linear patterns?

    - ✧ Yes → **decision tree** (automatically finds interactions and thresholds).

3. Find Patterns

Find Groups or Segments (Clustering)

Goal: Discover natural groupings (e.g., customer segments, product categories, or behavior clusters) in your observations.

- Is the data high-dimensional (many predictor variables)?

- ✧ Yes → Consider **dimensionality reduction first (principal component analysis [PCA], uniform manifold approximation and projection [UMAP]**), and then proceed to other.

- Do you know (approximately) how many groups exist?

  - ✧ Yes → Use **K-Means** or **Gaussian mixture models (GMM).**

    - *Context:* Use K-Means if you assume segments are roughly equal in "size" (circular). Use GMM if segments might be elongated or overlapping.

  - ✧ No → Use **hierarchical clustering** or **HDBSCAN.**

    - *Context:* Use hierarchical clustering if you need a "taxonomy" (e.g., there are sub-segments within segments). Use HDBSCAN if your data is "noisy" and you expect that some observations shouldn't belong to any group.

- Does the order of events matter? (For example, do you need to understand how groups or patterns evolve over time, like for customer churn or seasonal purchase cycles?)

  ✧ Yes → Use **sequential pattern mining** or **hidden Markov models (HMM).**

  - *Context:* Use these to identify the "typical path" a user takes before a specific outcome, like a conversion or a cancellation.

Find Anomalies (Anomaly Detection)

Goal: Detect outliers, fraud, defects, unusual behavior.

- Do you have labeled examples of "anomalies"?

  ✧ Yes → Use **random forest** or **XGBoost.**

- Are you looking for "needles in a haystack"?

  ✧ Yes → Use **isolation forest** or **local outlier factor (LOF).**

  - *Context:* Use isolation forest for global outliers (points far from everything). Use LOF for local outliers (points that are unusual compared only to their immediate neighbors).

- Are you trying to find anomalies in a time series?
    - ✧ Yes, and you're looking for simple spikes → Use **Z-Score**, **interquartile range (IQR)**, or **moving average**.
    - ✧ Yes, and your data is complex or has seasonal variability → Use **Prophet** or an **LSTM** (long short-term memory, a type of recurrent neural network).
- What is the "shape" of your data?
    - ✧ High dimensional (many features): Use **isolation forest**. It excels at "isolating" outliers.
    - ✧ Dense clusters: Use **local outlier factor (LOF)**. It identifies anomalies based on local density deviations compared to neighbors.
    - ✧ For other cases, try a **support vector machine (SVM)**. It finds a boundary that encompasses the bulk of the data and can be used to flag anything outside it.

Start simple, and increase complexity only if accuracy or performance demands it.

Find Key Drivers (Important Variables)

Goal: Determine which variables have the most significant impact on the model's output to inform business strategy, risk mitigation, or resource allocation.

- Do you have a target variable? If you have a defined outcome you are trying to predict (e.g., customer churn, credit risk, or equipment failure), you can use supervised methods to rank features.

    ✧ Yes → Use **feature importance methods.**

    - For a quick ranking → Use **random forest** or **gradient boosting.**
    - If you need rigorous statistical testing → **permutation importance** or **SHAP values.**

    ✧ Yes, and it needs to be fast → Use **decision tree**-based methods like random forest or gradient boosting (XGBoost, LightGBM, CatBoost).

    - *Mechanism*: These models provide internal "Gini importance" or "gain" metrics. They track how often a variable is used to split data and how much that split reduces uncertainty (impurity).

- *Best for*: Rapid prototyping and handling non-linear relationships without heavy preprocessing.

✧ No → Use **PCA** (to find which variables explain most variance) or **correlation analysis**.

- *Mechanism*: When you don't have a specific outcome to predict but want to understand the structure of your data and which variables carry the most "signal," PCA transforms variables into a new set of "components." By looking at the "loadings" on each component you can see which original variables contribute most to the variance in the dataset.
- *Best for:* Reducing noise and identifying the "essence" of a complex dataset.

Note: While these ML methods are powerful for finding predictive importance, they do not prove causality. A variable might be a "top driver" because it is a proxy for another hidden factor. Always validate your findings with domain experts before making material changes to business processes.

Make Recommendations

Goal: Suggest items to users (products, content, or connections).

- Do you have historical item-level interaction data (like clicks, purchases, or ratings)?
    - ✧ Yes → Use **collaborative filtering.**
        - If you need high scalability and simplicity → Use **matrix factorization (SVD or ALS).**
            - *Mechanism:* It breaks down a massive table of user-item interactions into smaller mathematical components ("vectors") to fill in the blanks of what a user might like next.
            - *Best for:* Large-scale retail or media platforms where you need a reliable, "tried and true" approach for "users who bought this also bought..." carousels.

- If context (time, location, or device) is critical to the sale → Use **factorization machines.**
    - *Mechanism:* It models interactions between variables, allowing the system to understand that a user's preference for "hot coffee" changes based on the "outside temperature" variable.
    - *Best for:* Food delivery apps, news aggregators, or seasonal e-commerce where the *when* and *where* are as important as the *what.*

- If you need maximum accuracy and have complex, multi-modal data → Use **deep learning.**
    - *Mechanism:* Uses multi-layered neural networks to find non-linear, "hidden" patterns in user behavior that traditional math might miss.
    - *Best for:* Social media feeds or high-frequency streaming services (like Netflix or TikTok) where capturing

subtle nuances in user behavior is the competitive advantage.

- ✧ No → Use **content-based filtering.**
  - *Mechanism:* This model ignores what other users are doing. It recommends items by matching the attributes of a product (e.g., color, category, author) to a user's explicit profile or past preferences.
  - *Best for:* New platforms with little data, or items with very rich metadata (like a library of technical papers or a specialized niche catalog).

- Does the business require high explainability?
  - ✧ Yes → Use **content-based filtering** or **collaborative filtering.**
    - *Mechanism:* These models allow for clear "Because you liked X..." logic. You can point to a specific feature (genre) or a specific neighbor (User B) as the reason for the suggestion.

- *Best for:* Financial services, healthcare, or any highly regulated industry where a "black box" recommendation could lead to legal or trust issues.

- ✧ No → Use **deep learning** or **hybrid models.**

  - *Mechanism:* These prioritize the "Click-Through Rate" above all else. They are highly accurate but the logic behind a specific recommendation is often buried deep within the model's layers.
  - *Best for:* General consumer retail or entertainment where the user cares more about the relevance of the suggestion than why it was made.

REFERENCES

Azevedo, Beatriz Flamia, Ana Maria AC Rocha, and Ana I. Pereira. "Hybrid approaches to optimization and machine learning methods: a systematic literature review." *Machine Learning* 113, no. 7 (2024): 4055-4097.

Harlalka, Rajat. "Choosing the Right Machine Learning Algorithm." HackerNoon, June 16, 2018. https://hackernoon.com/choosing-the-right-machine-learning-algorithm-68126944ce1f.

Jatana, V. (2019). Machine learning algorithms. In A. Panesar, *Machine Learning and AI for Healthcare,* 119-188. *https://doi.org/10.1007/978-1-4842-3799-1_4.*

CHAPTER 6

Model Evaluation

"When everything speeds up, discernment is the first casualty."

—Hiten Shah, CEO of Crazy Egg

In This Chapter

- Machine learning performance metrics help humans evaluate whether a model is ready for real-world use, while loss functions guide model training internally. This chapter focuses on the former.
- Different evaluation metrics are best suited for different ML tasks: prediction, classification, clustering, anomaly detection, and natural language processing (NLP).
- Choose your performance metric by considering the real-world consequences of different types of errors, not just overall accuracy.

What Is ML Evaluation?

Imagine you're learning to play a new sport. To get better, you need a coach to correct your form during practice, but you also need a scoreboard during the game to tell you if you are actually winning. In machine learning, *evaluation* is that scoreboard.

Performance metrics are a critical part of every machine learning project because they tell you if you are making progress. They put a concrete number on how well your model is achieving its goals. Whether you're building a simple prediction tool or a highly advanced algorithm, you (and your model) will need a specific metric to judge its performance.

Models use something called *loss function* internally, while you (the human evaluating the performance of the model overall) will select and consult a *performance metric*.

- **Loss functions** are like a strict coach during practice. A loss function is like a report card that tells an AI how wrong its answers are. The bigger the "loss" number, the worse it did. ML algorithms use this score to help the AI learn from its mistakes and get better over time, kind of like how you learn to shoot better in basketball by seeing how many shots you miss. Loss functions measure performance mathematically to help the model learn and adjust its internal settings (optimization) and are used by the model to evaluate itself.
- **Performance metrics** are like the final score. They monitor how well the model solves the problem in a way that humans can decide whether to use that model or not. While the loss function is what the AI uses to train itself, performance metrics tell us whether the AI is actually good at the task we care about, so we can decide if it's ready to be applied in the real world.

This chapter focuses on helping humans understand and choose appropriate performance metrics because I suspect there will be more humans than models reading this book.

Prediction (Regression)

In ML, *regression* just means predicting a specific number, like the price of a house or the temperature tomorrow. That number (called the *dependent variable*) can be predicted using a single *independent variable* or multiple independent variables. Because the predicted answer will be a number, we can evaluate these models by measuring the difference between what the answer was and what the model predicted.

Key evaluation metrics include:

1. **Mean absolute error (MAE):** This is the simplest measure. It calculates the average "distance" between the prediction and the reality. If the house costs $200,000 and the model predicts $205,000, the error is $5,000. MAE averages these errors. It is great because it doesn't exaggerate mistakes, but rather treats them directly as they are.

2. **Mean squared error (MSE):** This popular metric takes the difference between each observed value and actual value, *squares* each difference, and then averages those differences. By squaring the number, it penalizes big mistakes much more heavily than small ones.

3. **Root mean squared error (RMSE):** This is the square root of the MSE. It is used more often because it fixes a small issue with ordinary MSE: since MSE squares the differences between observed and actual values, the units become uninterpretable (like "dollars squared"). RMSE brings the number back to the original unit (dollars), making the metric easier to interpret, and easier to explain to a boss or a client.

4. **R2 (coefficient of determination):** This tells you how well your model explains the variability in the data you are modeling. An R^2 of 1.0 (100%) means your model explains all the variation in the data (a perfect fit), while 0 means it explains none of the variation.

5. **Adjusted R2:** A reported R^2 will increase as new independent variables are added. This can trick you into thinking the model is improving just because you added more variables, even if the model isn't really performing better. To fix this, use Adjusted R^2, which only goes up if the improvement is more real.

Evaluation Considerations

When evaluating these models, be sure to take into account:

- **Overfitting**: Explaining 100% of the variation (an R^2 of 1.0) isn't always good; it means you may be modeling the noise instead of the signal in your data. When presented with a new forecast to make, the model won't be able to generalize beyond your training data.

- **Outliers**: When choosing a performance metric, look at your "outliers," those data points that are wildly different from the rest. Because MSE squares errors, a single massive error can make the model's performance look terrible, even if the model was doing well most of the time. If you want a metric that isn't thrown off by a few crazy data points, MAE is more robust.

Classification

Classification is the process of grouping observations into buckets, like "cat vs. dog for classifying images or "spam vs. not spam" for classifying email. Since the answer is a category, not a number, we can't measure how close our prediction is to reality. Instead, we check to see whether the model picked the right bucket.

Evaluating a classifier often begins by constructing a confusion matrix to examine ground-truth category labels against model predictions. "Positive" is defined as having a particular category membership, whereas "negative" is defined as not belonging to that category, as shown in Figure 6.1.

- **True positive (TP):** Number of observations in the positive class predicted correctly.

- **True negative (TN):** Number of observations in the negative class predicted correctly.
- **False positive (FP):** Number of observations in the negative class predicted incorrectly (also called Type I error in statistics).
- **False negative (FN):** Number of observations in the positive class predicted incorrectly (also called Type II error in statistics).

Test Results	**You Really Do Have a Serious Disease**	**You Don't have a Serious Disease**
You Have a Serious Disease	True Positives (TP)	False Positives (FP)
You Don't Have a Serious Disease	False Negatives (FN)	True Negatives (TN)

Figure 6.1 Example of a confusion matrix to evaluate a classifier that predicts a serious disease.

KEY EVALUATION METRICS

1. **Accuracy [correct classifications / total classifications]:** While simple, this performance metric can be misleading when the cost of misclassification is high or when membership in a particular category is rare (called *imbalanced classes*).

2. **Precision [TP / (TP + FP)]:** This answers the question: "Out of all the items we classified into our target group, how many were classified accurately?" Imagine a model identifying cancer. Precision asks: "Of the patients the model said had cancer, how many actually had it?"

3. **Sensitivity [TP / (TP + FP)]:** Also referred to as *true positive rate* (by data scientists), *recall* (by engineers); *sensitivity* is typically referenced in clinical settings. This asks the opposite question from precision: "Of the patients who actually have cancer, how many did our model find?"

4. **Specificity [TN / (TN + FP)]:** This measures how good the model is at identifying the negatives. It asks: "If you *don't* have cancer, how likely is it that the model knows that?"

5. **F1 Score [2TP / (2TP + FP + FN)]:** When it is important to accurately classify positives *and* negatives, this balanced score combines precision and recall into a single metric. High F1 indicates high precision and high recall. By plotting precision and recall on a chart with F1 as the contour, it is easier to evaluate the tradeoffs between different classifiers.

6. **Receiver operating characteristic (ROC/AUC)** [shown in Figure 6.2]: Unlike the previous metrics, which rely on a single decision threshold,

this plots false positive rate on the horizontal axis with true positive rate on the vertical axis to evaluate those metrics jointly. The Area Under the Curve (AUC) summarizes this performance into a single number between 0 and 1. It asks: "How effectively can the model distinguish between the two categories, regardless of where the decision line is drawn?" An AUC of 0.5 (case C in Figure 6.2) suggests the classification model is no better than a coin toss, while an AUC nearing 1.0 (case A in Figure 6.2) indicates that observations in each category can be perfectly distinguished from one another.

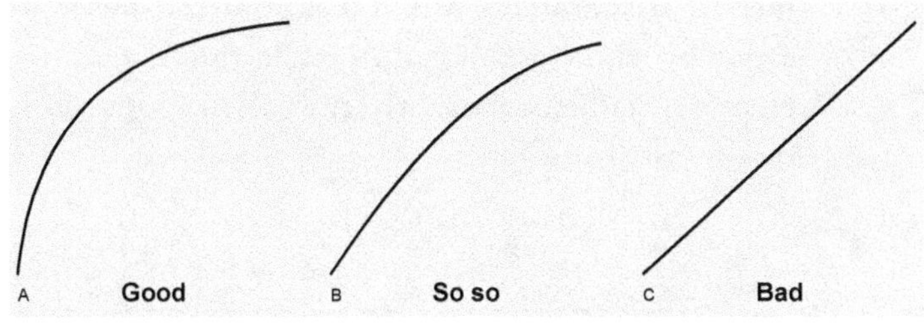

Figure 6.2 How to evaluate ROC curves by estimating AUC (Powers, 2011).

1. **Log loss [-(y Log p + (1-y) Log(1-p))]:** This metric for classifier accuracy examines each classification in terms of whether it was classified into the positive group (y=1 for yes) and the probability our model assigned to represent its

confidence in that binary prediction (p). Log loss, which is the sum of these values across all observations, applies a penalty for false classifications and ranges from zero to +∞. A perfect classifier has a log loss of zero. In a two-group classification task where membership in one category is not rare, a log loss < 0.693 reflects a classifier that is performing better than random guessing.

2. **Matthews correlation coefficient (MCC)** [shown in Figure 6.3]: This performance metric is computed from counts in a confusion matrix. It ranges from -1 (perfect misclassification) to +1 (perfect classification), with 0 indicating classification by random chance. As a result, this score reports overall model quality across all four confusion matrix categories.

$$MCC = \frac{TN \times TP - FN \times FP}{\sqrt{(TP + FP)(TP + FN)(TN + FP)(TN + FN)}}$$

Figure 6.3 Computing the Matthews correlation coefficient (MCC) from a confusion matrix.

EVALUATION STEPS AND CONSIDERATIONS

In scenarios with imbalanced classes, accuracy is a poor metric. A model might achieve high accuracy simply by predicting the dominant class, while failing to identify the minority class (meaning it has low recall). In these cases, F1 score, "balanced accuracy" (average recall of each class), or MCC are preferred.

Anomaly Detection

Anomaly detection involves identifying rare items or events that differ significantly from the majority of the data. This is closely related to binary classification but deals specifically with uncommon events.

KEY EVALUATION CONCEPTS

1. **Sensitivity/recall/true positive rate:** This is the critical metric for anomaly detection. It measures the likelihood that the test will detect the anomaly in an observation that is confirmed to have that anomaly.
2. **Type I vs. Type II errors:** You need to balance these two types of errors in anomaly detection scenarios.
    - **Type I (false positive):** The likelihood of detecting an anomaly when one does not exist (i.e., rejecting the null hypothesis). This is the "false

alarm" where you inaccurately identify an issue (e.g., the bank freezes your credit card as you're attempting to make a legitimate purchase).

- **Type II (false negative):** The likelihood of missing an anomaly when one is present (i.e., not rejecting the null hypothesis when it should have been rejected). This is the missed detection where you fail to spot the problem (e.g. a thief uses your credit card and the bank lets it go through).

EVALUATION STEPS AND CONSIDERATIONS

- Because anomalies are rare, datasets are inherently imbalanced. Standard accuracy is deceptive here. If 99% of data is normal, a model predicting "normal" for every instance achieves 99% accuracy but fails to detect 100% of anomalies.
- Metrics must focus on the minority class. To curb the rate of false negatives or false positives, techniques like oversampling (using algorithms like SMOTE to synthetically create new observations from the underrepresented group) or under-sampling (deleting observations from the group that is overrepresented) can be used during training.

PRACTICAL FOCUS

Anomaly detection cases are often associated with psychological and reputational risk, and you'll need to consider the reactions people will have to detecting an anomaly, and the actions that might be taken because of it.

Think about detecting a serious communicable disease, like measles. With an inaccurate detection, you might scare a healthy patient, or cause them to undergo treatment that is emotionally, physically, and financially costly. With a false negative, you risk releasing a contagious patient into the public, which could be catastrophic. In this case, you evaluate the model by keeping false negatives as close to zero as possible.

Clustering

In clustering, the goal is to uncover which observations are similar to other observations. Unlike classification, there are often no ground-truth labels during training, and the results must be examined by experts to determine utility. Quantitative performance metrics can complement this approach if you know to which clusters a subset of observations belong.

KEY EVALUATION METRICS

1. **Rand index:** This metric measures how often your clustering algorithm makes the same grouping decisions as the true labels. It counts all pairs of observations and checks whether your algorithm correctly placed them together in the same cluster or correctly separated them

into different clusters, then divides by the total number of pairs to get a score between 0 and 1.

2. **Silhouette coefficient:** This measures how well-separated your clusters are by comparing how close each observation is to others in its own cluster versus observations in neighboring clusters. For each observation, you calculate the average distance to members of its cluster and to the nearest other cluster, then combine these into a score between -1 and 1, where higher values mean tighter, more distinct clusters.
3. **Fowlkes-Mallows index (FMI)** [shown in Figure 6.4]: This metric measures the agreement between your clustering results and the true labels by focusing on pairs of observations that are grouped together. It calculates the geometric mean of precision (what fraction of pairs you grouped together actually belong together) and recall (what fraction of pairs that belong together you successfully grouped), producing a score between 0 and 1.

$$FMI = \frac{TP}{\sqrt{(TP + FP)(TP + FN)}}$$

Figure 6.4 Computing the FMI from a confusion matrix.

EVALUATION STEPS AND CONSIDERATIONS

Evaluation involves determining how well the ML model separates distinct groups. In practice, an iterative approach is often taken, combining observation and experience to find natural groupings in the data.

PRACTICAL FOCUS

Clustering is used to discover structure. In practical applications, evaluation is often based on the utility of the resulting clusters for downstream tasks (e.g., does a customer segmentation obtained through clustering help us meet distinct customer needs more effectively?).

Natural Language Processing (NLP)

Because NLP handles such a broad collection of tasks, results are evaluated in many ways. NLP results can often be treated like classification tasks (e.g. determining the sentiment of a word or sentence, classifying groups of documents into topics).

KEY EVALUATION METRICS

Here are some examples of evaluation techniques for a variety of NLP tasks:

- For **classification**: accuracy, precision, and F1
- For **information synthesis**: ROUGE (compares a summary to a benchmark summary)
- For **machine translation**: BLEU (compares a model's output to a translation benchmark)

- For **speech recognition**: word error rate (WER), character error rate (CER)
- For **predicting text**: Perplexity

EVALUATION STEPS AND CONSIDERATIONS

When we use NLP for things like sentiment analysis (is this tweet happy or sad?), we treat it like a classification problem.

- **Precision**: Of the documents the computer selected, what proportion were actually the ones we wanted?
- **Recall**: Did the model find all the relevant documents, or did it miss some?

In a document retrieval scenario (like a Google search), these performance metrics are also relevant. For example, if you search for "apple pie recipes" and get ten documents back, but only five are legitimate recipes, the precision of that retrieval is 50%. If there were one hundred apple pie recipes on the entire internet and it only found five, the recall is very low.

PRACTICAL FOCUS

To select the best evaluation metric, consider the intention and the risks around your task. If the goal of a sentiment analysis is to flag negative customer reviews, recall is likely the best option (to ensure no negative feedback is missed). If the goal is to auto-publish positive reviews, precision should be the priority (to ensure no negative review is accidentally published).

REFERENCES

Erickson, Bradley J., and Felipe Kitamura. "Magician's corner: 9. Performance metrics for machine learning models." Radiology: *Artificial Intelligence 3*, no. 3 (2021): e200126.

Powers, David MW. "Evaluation: from precision, recall and F-measure to ROC, informedness, markedness and correlation." arXiv preprint arXiv:2010.16061 (2020).

Varoquaux, Gaël, and Olivier Colliot. "Evaluating machine learning models and their diagnostic value." Machine learning for brain disorders (2023): 601-630.

METHOD 1

Linear Regression

DESCRIPTION

Regression is a **supervised** machine learning algorithm: it learns from labeled data (predictors paired with known outcomes) by finding the best-fit line or hyperplane that maps inputs to outputs. It finds the mathematical relationship between inputs (predictors) and an output (response), allowing you to estimate the output for new, unseen input values. You *can* do linear regression with pencil and paper with limited data, but this is impractical with large datasets. Linear regression is also considered a supervised machine learning algorithm: it learns from labeled data (predictors paired with known outcomes) by finding the best-fit line or hyperplane that maps inputs to outputs.

HOW IT WORKS

- **This method finds the straight line** that best fits your data points. The equation takes the form $y = \beta_0 + \beta_1 x_1 + \beta_2 x_2 + \dots + \beta_n x_n$ where y is the predicted output, x are the input variables, and β are the coefficients for each input that explain how much y changes when x increases by one unit. β_0 is the intercept (the value of y when all x is equal to zero).
- **This method works because** squaring distances ensures that positive and negative errors are treated

equally while penalizing large errors more heavily than small ones, resulting in a line that best balances all deviations from the data.

- **Use linear regression** when you have historical data showing the relationship between inputs and the output you want to predict, and you suspect that the relationship between inputs and outputs is linear.

WHAT TO USE IT FOR

In quality improvement contexts, consider regression for:

- **Understanding relationships:** Determining which process variables have the strongest influence on quality outcomes. Quantify how much a one-unit change in an input affects the output. Identify which factors matter most and which can be safely ignored.
- **Predicting process outcomes:** Estimating cycle time based on batch size, temperature, and operator experience. Forecast defect rates from process parameters. Predict customer satisfaction scores from service delivery metrics.
- **Optimizing processes:** Finding the combination of settings that minimizes defects or maximizes yield. Establish target values for controllable inputs to achieve desired outputs.
- **Setting specifications:** Using the relationship between process variables and outcomes to establish reasonable control limits and tolerances.

Depending on the nature of the problem you need to solve, there are many specialized regression techniques to choose from. When your predictors are noisy or overlap with each other, consider Ridge regression (which prevents any single predictor from dominating the model) or Lasso regression (which drops unimportant variables entirely, giving you a simpler model). When the relationship isn't linear, consider polynomial regression or spline regression.

HOW TO USE IT

Step 1: Prepare Your Data

Gather historical observations that include both the outcome you want to predict and the potential predictor values. Check your data quality: look for missing values, recording errors, and extreme outliers that might skew results. Aim for at least 15–30 observations per predictor variable.

Step 2: Explore Relationships Visually

Before fitting any model, create scatterplots of each predictor against the outcome. Look for linear patterns, non-linearity, outliers, and clusters.

Step 3: Check Assumptions

Before creating your model, verify:

1. **Linearity.** The relationship between predictor and response is linear. Plot residuals against fitted values—you should see no clear pattern.

2. **Independence.** Observations should not depend on each other. This matters especially for time series data, where autocorrelation can be a problem.

3. **No significant outliers.** Extreme values can disproportionately affect results. Cook's distance and leverage plots help identify these.

4. **Accurate measurement.** Ensure you have reliable instruments and techniques for data collection.

After building your model, examine the residuals (differences between predicted and actual values), ideally through plots. If assumptions are violated, consider transformations, robust regression methods, or alternative models.

Step 4: Fit the Model

You can use statistical software like R, spreadsheet tools in Excel or Google Sheets, or AI assistants like Claude, Gemini, or ChatGPT. Write a prompt asking the AI to generate regression code and interpret the results (see Figures M1.1 and M1.2 for examples). Always verify that the AI interpreted your data and instructions correctly.

Here is data representing height in inches, age in years, and weight in pounds. The first element in each group corresponds to the first person, while the second element in each group corresponds to the second person, and so on for each of the 14 people we sampled. Write code to perform a multiple linear regression to help us predict weight using both height and age as predictors. Return the regression equation, the key findings from the regression in a clearly labeled table, model fit as described by R^2, Adjusted R^2, and the F-statistic, and a short interpretation of the results for each predictor.

The data is:
heights_inches = (60,69,72,75,66,64,62,68,68,70,56,66,65,64)
age_years = (22,28,32,40,25,45,30,32,45,38,22,26,34,35)
weight_pounds = (130,150,180,210,155,100,110,140,160,185,105,120,155,145)

Figure M1.1 A prompt to claude.ai to request a multiple linear regression on sampled data.

REGRESSION EQUATION

Weight = -224.13 + 5.84(Height) – 0.48(Age)

KEY REGRESSION FINDINGS

Predictor	Coefficient	Std Error	t-value	p-value	95% CI
Intercept	-224.13	71.43	-3.14	0.0094	[-381.35, -66.91]
Height	5.84	1.22	4.79	<0.001	[3.15, 8.52]
Age	-0.48	0.78	-0.61	0.5565	[-2.20, 1.25]

MODEL FIT STATISTICS

Metric	Value
R^2	0.7124
Adjusted R^2	0.6601
F-statistic	13.62
F-statistic p-value	0.0011
Degrees of Freedom	(2, 11)

Figure M1.2 Results from prompting claude.ai to execute multiple linear regression.

INTERPRETATION

Overall Model: The regression model is statistically significant ($F(2, 11) = 13.62$, $p = 0.001$). Height and age together explain 71.2% of the variance in weight ($R^2 = 0.71$). After adjusting for the number of predictors, 66.0% of variance is explained.

Height: Height is a **statistically significant** predictor ($t = 4.79$, $p < 0.001$). For each 1-inch increase in height, weight increases by approximately 5.84 pounds, holding age constant. This is the primary driver of weight prediction in this model.

Age: Age is **not statistically significant** ($t = -0.61$, $p = 0.56$). The negative coefficient (-0.48) suggests a slight decrease in weight with age, but this relationship is not reliable given the high p-value. The 95% confidence interval spans both negative and positive values, indicating age does not contribute meaningfully to predicting weight in this sample.

Figure M1.2 Results from prompting claude.ai to execute multiple linear regression. (continued)

INTERPRETING RESULTS

Check your model's assumptions: Residuals are the gaps between what your model predicted and what happened in reality. Plot them and look for random scatter around zero. If you see curves or funnel shapes, your model may need adjustment.

Variance should stay consistent across your data. If the spread of residuals widens or narrows as values increase, your predictions will be less reliable at certain ranges.

Normal distribution of residuals matters mainly when you're making statistical inferences. With large datasets, this becomes less of a concern.

Understand your key metrics: R^2 (R-squared) tells you how much of the outcome your model explains. An R^2 of 0.70 means your predictors account for 70% of the variation in your data. The remaining 30% comes from factors you haven't measured or random noise.

What counts as "good" depends on context. Lab experiments might expect 0.9 or higher. In complex business or human systems, 0.30–0.50 can still be valuable. For models with multiple predictors, use Adjusted R^2, which accounts for model complexity.

P-values indicate whether a predictor is statistically meaningful. Values below 0.05 suggest significance; predictors with high p-values may not be contributing much.

Coefficients show the relationship between each predictor and your outcome. A coefficient of 5 means that for every one-unit increase in that predictor, the outcome increases by 5 units (holding everything else constant). Negative coefficients indicate inverse relationships.

Important caveats: A high R^2 shows association, not causation. Two variables may move together because of a third factor, not because one drives the other. Don't rely on any single metric. Consider your results as a whole. Remove predictors that aren't statistically significant and rerun the model. If possible, test your final model on fresh data to see how well it generalizes. Document your equation and performance metrics for future reference.

LIMITATIONS AND PITFALLS

Correlation ≠ causation: Strong relationships don't prove one variable causes another. Confounding variables may be responsible; only experiments establish causality.

Extrapolation is dangerous: Models only work within the data range used to build them. Predictions beyond this range are unreliable.

Check outliers: Single unusual points can dramatically skew results, especially at extreme values. Always examine scatterplots.

Account for non-linearity: Linear regression assumes straight-line relationships. Curved patterns will cause systematic prediction errors—check residual plots.

Multicollinearity: Highly correlated predictors make individual coefficients unstable and hard to interpret.

Overfitting: Too many predictors relative to sample size create models that fit historical data but predict poorly. Use Adjusted R^2 and validation data.

METHOD 2

Regularized Linear Regression

DESCRIPTION

Regularized linear regression is a **supervised** machine learning algorithm for prediction, designed to improve the reliability of predictions based on complex or "noisy" datasets. While standard linear regression finds the best-fit line by minimizing the differences between observed and predicted values, regularized regression adds a *penalty* to the model to prevent overfitting (where a model fits historical data perfectly but can't predict new, unseen outcomes well). This method is particularly useful when you have many predictors that may overlap or when some variables are not truly important to the outcome. By "shrinking" the influence of less important variables, regularization produces more stable models that generalize better to the real world.

HOW IT WORKS

Standard regression works by minimizing the sum of the squared distances between data points and the regression line. Regularization modifies this objective by adding a **penalty term** to the mathematical equation.

The two primary types of regularization are **lasso** and **ridge:**

- **Lasso regression ("L1 regularization"):** Adds a penalty equal to the absolute value of the magnitude of coefficients. This technique has the unique ability to shrink unimportant coefficients to zero, effectively selecting the best predictors for you.

- **Ridge regression ("L2 regularization"):** Adds a penalty equal to the square of the magnitude of coefficients to prevent any one predictor from dominating the model while considering all inputs.

The penalty weight (λ): Think of this as a "complexity dial" that you can use to control how strictly to restrain your model (see Table M1). In a standard linear regression, there is zero penalty for large or complex coefficients. But when you increase the penalty, you are telling the model: "I want you to fit the data, but I will penalize you if you make the coefficients too big." Large coefficients are not desirable: even a tiny change in that input variable creates a massive swing in the predicted output. This makes your model hypersensitive to the random fluctuations of noise.

Value of λ	Model Behavior	Result
λ = 0	Standard linear regression. The model focuses solely on minimizing error.	Highest risk of overfitting. Coefficients may be unnaturally large to fit every data point.
Low λ	A small penalty is applied so the model starts to prioritize simpler relationships.	Highest risk of overfitting. Coefficients may be unnaturally large to fit every data point.

Table M1 The effects of tuning the penalty weight λ.

Value of λ	Model Behavior	Result
High λ	A heavy penalty is applied. Large coefficients become very "expensive" for the model.	Coefficients shrink significantly. In Lasso, unimportant variables are forced to be zero.
Infinite λ	The penalty is so high that no predictor is "worth" the cost.	All coefficients (except the intercept) become zero, resulting in a flat line. This is not something you would choose for modeling.

Table M1 The effects of tuning the penalty weight λ. (continued)

WHAT TO USE IT FOR

In quality improvement and process work, regularized regression is essential for:

- **Managing multicollinearity:** When your predictors are highly correlated (e.g., temperature and pressure in a closed system), standard regression coefficients become unstable. Ridge regression stabilizes these values.
- **High-dimensional data:** When the number of potential factors (predictors) is large relative to your sample size, this can lead to overfitting.
- **Feature selection:** Use Lasso regression to identify which factors truly matter most and which ones can be safely ignored by dropping them from the model.

- **Improving generalization:** Use when you need a model that will perform reliably on fresh data rather than just fitting the historical data used to build it.

HOW TO USE IT

Step 1: Prepare and Standardize Your Data

Gather your historical observations. In standard linear regression, the model doesn't care if one variable is measured in miles and another in inches; it just adjusts the coefficients to account for the scale. In contrast, regularized regression adds a penalty based on the size of those coefficients, so the scale of your data suddenly matters a great deal. Standardization (also known as Z-score normalization) transforms your variables so they share a common scale with a mean of 0 and a standard deviation of 1. This ensures that your regularization penalty is applied fairly across all predictors, regardless of their original units. To standardize, convert each input variable to its z-score.

Step 2: Choose Method and Tune Hyperparameter (λ)

Choose Ridge regression when most predictors have small, distributed effects and you want variables kept. Choose Lasso when you suspect only a few variables are actually important, and you want the unimportant predictors automatically removed. Next, find the best value for your hyperparameter, the penalty weight. This is usually done via cross-validation, where the AI or software tests different penalty values on subsets of your data to see which one produces the lowest prediction error on new ones.

Step 3: Check Assumptions

Before creating your model, verify:

1. **A binary outcome.** Your desired output should have exactly two categories which can be structured as (Group 1/Group 2) or (Group 1/Not Group 1).
2. **Independence.** Observations should *not* depend on each other (like before and after measurements on the same person).
3. **No extreme multicollinearity exists.** Predictors should not be highly correlated with each other (like height and weight, because taller people typically weigh more than shorter people, overall).
4. **Linearity in log-odds.** The relationship between continuous predictors and the log-odds of the outcome should be approximately linear.
5. **Adequate sample size.** You need enough observations in your training data for the category with the less-common outcome. If one category is only represented in a small portion of your inputs, you may need to choose an alternative algorithm that works well for *imbalanced classes.*

Step 4: Fit the Model

Use statistical software like R or AI assistants like Claude, Gemini, or ChatGPT. Ask the assistant to write and execute code to generate your model in a language with trusted data science capabilities like Python. Always independently verify that the AI interpreted your data and instructions correctly (Figures M2.1 and M2.2).

> I have a dataset from a manufacturing process where we are measuring **Yield (in grams)** based on three predictors: **Temperature** (°C), **Pressure** (PSI), and **Humidity** (%). I want to see whether **Ridge (L2) or Lasso (L1) regression** can be used to handle potential overfitting and high correlation between variables.
>
> Please write and execute Python code to:
>
> 1. Perform a **Standard Scaler** transformation (crucial for regularization).
> 2. Fit a **Ridge (or Lasso)** regression model.
> 3. Calculate the **Mean Squared Error (MSE)** and **R-squared (R^2)**.
> 4. Provide a table comparing the **Original Coefficients** vs. the **Regularized Coefficients**.
> 5. Briefly explain how the regularization changed the impact of the predictors.

Figure M2.1 A prompt to gemini.google.com (Gemini 3) to request regularized regression on sampled data.

The Data (20 samples):

- **Temperature:** [22, 25, 23, 28, 24, 25, 29, 21, 22, 26, 27, 24, 23, 22, 28, 26, 25, 24, 21, 23]
- **Pressure:** [101, 103, 102, 108, 104, 105, 109, 101, 102, 106, 107, 104, 103, 101, 108, 105, 105, 104, 101, 102]
- **Humidity:** [45, 48, 46, 55, 47, 49, 58, 44, 45, 52, 54, 48, 47, 45, 56, 51, 50, 48, 44, 46]
- **Yield (Target):** [150, 155, 153, 165, 158, 159, 170, 148, 151, 162, 164, 157, 154, 151, 168, 161, 160, 158, 149, 153]"

Figure M2.1 A prompt to gemini.google.com (Gemini 3) to request regularized regression on sampled data. (continued)

To analyze the impact of regularization on your manufacturing dataset, I performed a standard scaling of the predictors and compared **Ordinary Least Squares (OLS)** regression with **Ridge (L2)** regression.

Model Performance Metrics

The following metrics compare the performance of the unregularized model (OLS) against the Ridge model on the scaled dataset.

Figure M2.2 Results from prompting gemini.google.com (Gemini 3) to execute logistic regression.

Metric	Original (OLS)	Ridge (L2)
Mean Squared Error (MSE)	0.6798	0.7793
R-squared	0.9823	0.9797

Coefficient Comparison Table

Regularization penalizes the magnitude of the coefficients. Below is the comparison of the weights assigned to each standardized predictor:

Predictor	Original (OLS) Coeff	Ridge (L2) Coeff
Temperature (°C)	2.1254	1.9337
Pressure (PSI)	4.1545	2.6483
Humidity (%)	-0.1020	1.4891

Figure M2.2 Results from prompting gemini.google.com (Gemini 3) to execute logistic regression. (continued)

Analysis of Regularization Impact

1. **Handling Multicollinearity**: In the original OLS model, Humidity had a slightly negative coefficient (-0.102). However, in the Ridge model, it became significantly positive (1.489). This suggests that the predictors (Temperature, Pressure, and Humidity) are highly correlated. OLS can produce unstable and counter-intuitive coefficients when features are redundant; Ridge stabilizes this by distributing the "importance" more evenly across the correlated variables.

2. **Reduction of Sensitivity**: The coefficient for Pressure was reduced significantly (from 4.15 to 2.65). By shrinking these large coefficients, Ridge regression makes the model less sensitive to small fluctuations in any single variable, which helps prevent **overfitting**.

3. **Trade-off**: You will notice the MSE is slightly higher and R2 is slightly lower for the Ridge model. This is a classic "bias-variance tradeoff." While the Ridge model fits the training data slightly less perfectly than OLS, it is generally more robust and likely to perform better on new, unseen data from your manufacturing line.

Figure M2.2 Results from prompting gemini.google.com (Gemini 3) to execute logistic regression. (continued)

INTERPRETING RESULTS

When reviewing the output of a regularized model, focus on how the coefficients have changed compared to a standard model. You'll see:

- **Coefficient shrinkage.** Notice that coefficients will generally be smaller than the ones you get from standard linear regression. This represents the "cost" of making the model more stable.
- **Zeroed variables (Lasso).** If you used Lasso, look for predictors with a coefficient of exactly zero. These are the variables the model has determined are not contributing meaningful information.
- **Validation error.** Look for the "mean squared error" (MSE) on the test set. If the regularized model has a lower test error than the standard model, it is a better predictor, even if the R^2 on the training data is slightly lower.
- **Bias-variance tradeoff.** By adding a penalty, you are intentionally introducing a small amount of "bias" to significantly reduce "variance" (unreliability). A "good" model balances these two.

LIMITATIONS AND PITFALLS

- **Loss of interpretability:** In Ridge regression, because all variables are kept, it can sometimes be harder to explain the exact real-world impact of a single unit change.

- **Underfitting:** If the penalty metric is too high, the model will be too simple and miss important patterns in the data. This leads to poor performance for both historical and new data.
- **Arbitrary selection:** In Lasso, if two predictors are highly correlated, the model might pick one at random to keep and set the other to zero, which can be misleading if you are trying to understand causal relationships.
- **Data scaling:** Forgetting to scale or standardize your data before running regularization will lead to incorrect penalties and invalid results.

METHOD 3

Logistic Regression

DESCRIPTION

This supervised machine learning technique for **classification** learns from labeled data (predictors paired with known categorical outcomes) by finding the best decision boundary that separates the classes. Unlike linear regression, which predicts continuous values, logistic regression predicts the probability that an observation belongs to a particular category. These can be pass/fail, defective/non-defective, yes/no, and similar groupings. The algorithm produces a probability between 0 and 1, which you then convert to a class prediction using a threshold value between 0 and 1.

HOW IT WORKS

- This method transforms a linear combination of inputs into a probability using an S-shaped (sigmoid) function. The equation takes the form $p = 1 / (1 + e^{-z})$ where $z = \beta_0 + \beta_1 x_1 + \beta_2 x_2 + ... + \beta_n x_n$. Here p is the predicted probability, x are input variables, and β are the coefficients the algorithm learns from your observations. β_0 is the intercept.
- This method works because the sigmoid function naturally forces outputs to be between 0 and 1, making it ideal for probability estimation. The model finds coefficients that maximize the likelihood of observing

your actual data by identifying the parameters that make your observed outcomes most probable.

- Use logistic regression when you have historical data showing the relationship between inputs and a categorical outcome you want to predict, particularly when you need to understand *which factors influence the probability of an event* and *by how much*.

WHAT TO USE IT FOR

In quality improvement contexts, consider logistic regression for:

- Predicting binary outcomes
    - ✧ Estimating whether a product will pass or fail inspection based on process parameters
    - ✧ Forecasting whether a patient will respond to treatment
    - ✧ Predicting whether a customer will churn based on service metrics
- Understanding risk factors
    - ✧ Determining which process variables most strongly influence the probability of a defect occurring

  - ✧ Quantifying how much a one-unit change in an input affects the likelihood of the outcome
  - ✧ Identifying which factors to prioritize for intervention

- Setting thresholds and triggers
  - ✧ Establishing alert levels for process parameters that signal elevated risk
  - ✧ Creating decision rules for when to inspect, intervene, or escalate

- Resource allocation
  - ✧ Prioritizing which cases need attention based on predicted probability of adverse outcomes
  - ✧ Targeting quality interventions where they will have the greatest impact

For outcomes with more than two categories, you have a choice: set the output variable to reflect membership in your category or not (hot dog/not hot dog) or consider **multinomial logistic regression**. When categories have a natural order (e.g., low/medium/high risk), **ordinal logistic regression** may be more appropriate.

HOW TO USE IT

Step 1: Prepare Your Data

Gather historical observations that include both the binary outcome you want to predict and the potential predictor values. Make sure one of your variables reflects which category the observation is associated with (e.g. YES/NO or 1/0). Check for missing values, measurement errors, and recording errors. Aim for at least 10–20 observations per predictor variable, and make sure both of your outcomes are sufficiently represented.

Step 2: Explore Relationships Visually

Create boxplots comparing predictor distributions between outcome groups. Look for separation between classes: predictors showing *clear* differences between groups will likely be useful. Check for outliers that might unduly influence results.

Step 3: Check Assumptions

Before creating your model, verify:

1. **Binary outcome.** Your desired output should have exactly two categories which can be structured as (Group 1/ Group 2) or (Group 1/Not Group 1).

2. **Independence.** Observations should *not* depend on each other (like before and after measurements on the same person).

3. **No extreme multicollinearity.** Predictors should not be highly correlated with each other

(like height and weight, because taller people typically weigh more than shorter people, overall).

4. **Linearity in log-odds.** The relationship between continuous predictors and the log-odds of the outcome should be approximately linear.

5. **Adequate sample size.** You need a sufficient number of observations in your training data for the category with the less common outcome. If one category is only represented in a small portion of your inputs, you may need to choose an alternative algorithm that works well for *imbalanced classes.*

Step 4: Fit the Model

You can use statistical software like R, spreadsheet tools in Excel or Google Sheets, or AI assistants like Claude, Gemini, or ChatGPT. Write a prompt asking the AI to generate logistic regression code and interpret the results (see Figures M3.1 and M3.2 for examples). Always verify that the AI interpreted your data and instructions correctly.

Here is data representing temperature in Celsius, pressure in PSI, and whether each batch passed quality inspection (1=pass, 0=fail). The first element in each group corresponds to the first batch, and so on for each of the 20 batches we sampled. Write code to perform logistic regression to help us predict pass/fail using both temperature and pressure as predictors. Return the regression equation, the key findings in a clearly labeled table, model fit metrics including accuracy, and a short interpretation of the results for each predictor.

The data is:
temperature_celsius = (150,155,160,165,170,152,158,163,168,173,151,156,161,166,171,154,159,164,169,174)
pressure_psi = (30,32,31,33,35,29,31,32,34,36,28,30,31,33,34,30,32,33,35,37)
passed_inspection = (0,0,1,1,1,0,0,1,1,1,0,0,0,1,1,0,1,1,1,1)

Figure M3.1 A prompt to claude.ai Opus 4.5 to request logistic regression on sampled data.

REGRESSION EQUATION

logit(P) = -281.19 + (1.03 × Temperature) + (3.74 × Pressure)

Or in probability form: P(Pass) = 1 / (1 + e^(-(-281.19 + 1.03×Temp + 3.74×Pressure)))

KEY FINDINGS - COEFFICIENT TABLE

Variable	Coefficient	Std Error	z-value	p-value	Odds Ratio
Intercept	-281.19	237.67	-1.18	0.237	N/A
Temperature (°C)	1.03	0.86	1.19	0.234	2.80
Pressure (PSI)	3.74	3.78	0.99	0.322	42.28

MODEL FIT METRICS

Metric	Value
Accuracy	0.9500 (95.0%)
Log-Likelihood	-2.2778
Null Log-Likelihood	-13.4602
Pseudo R-squared (McFadden)	0.8308
AIC	10.5556
BIC	13.5428
Sensitivity	(True Positive Rate) 1.0000
Specificity	(True Negative Rate) 0.8750

Figure M3.2 Results from prompting claude.ai Opus 4.5 to execute logistic regression.

INTERPRETATION

Temperature: Each 1°C increase multiplies the odds of passing by ~2.80. Higher temperatures are associated with increased likelihood of passing, though the effect is not statistically significant at $p<0.05$ (likely due to small sample size and multicollinearity with pressure).

Pressure: Each 1 PSI increase multiplies the odds of passing by ~42.28—a strong effect suggesting pressure is highly influential. However, like temperature, it doesn't reach statistical significance ($p=0.32$) given the sample size.

Overall: Despite non-significant individual predictors, the model performs excellently with 95% accuracy and explains 83% of the variance. Both variables work together to predict quality outcomes, with higher temperature and pressure combinations strongly associated with passing inspection. The lack of statistical significance is likely due to the small sample ($n=20$) and correlation between the two predictors.

Figure M3.2 Results from prompting claude.ai Opus 4.5 to execute logistic regression. (continued)

INTERPRETING RESULTS

Understand odds ratios. Unlike linear regression coefficients, logistic regression coefficients represent changes in log-odds, which is not intuitive for most people (including the author). Convert them to odds ratios by exponentiating $e(_b)$. An odds ratio of 1.5 means that for each one-unit increase in that predictor, the odds of the outcome occurring multiply by 1.5 (a 50% increase in odds). Ratios below 1 indicate decreased odds.

Evaluate model performance. Accuracy alone can be misleading, especially in a situation with imbalanced classes. Also examine sensitivity (true positive rate), specificity (true negative rate), and AUC-ROC (area under the receiver operating characteristic curve). AUC ranges from 0.5 (no discrimination) to 1.0 (perfect discrimination); values above 0.7 are generally acceptable, and above 0.8 is good.

Assess statistical significance. P-values below 0.05 suggest a predictor may reliably contribute to the model. Confidence intervals for odds ratios that don't cross 1.0 indicate statistical significance.

Check calibration. A well-calibrated model's predicted probabilities should match or nearly match observed frequencies. If you predict 70% probability for a group of observations, approximately 70% of them should actually *have* the outcome.

LIMITATIONS AND PITFALLS

Class imbalance: When one classification is rare (e.g., a 5% defect rate), the model may tend to predict the majority class. Work with imbalance classes by studying resampling techniques, adjusted thresholds, or class-weighted models.

Linearity assumption: Logistic regression assumes a linear relationship between predictors and log-odds. Non-linear relationships require transformations or different models.

Complete separation: When a predictor *perfectly* separates outcomes, coefficient estimates become infinite and unreliable. This can occur with small samples or many predictors.

Correlation ≠ causation: As with linear regression, associations don't prove causality.

Threshold sensitivity: A 0.5 probability threshold may not be optimal for your problem context. Adjust based on the relative costs of false positives versus false negatives.

Overfitting: Too many predictors relative to sample size (especially relative to events in the smaller outcome class) creates models that don't generalize. Techniques like regularization or cross-validation are typically used to detect and prevent this.

METHOD 4

Decision Trees

DESCRIPTION

A decision tree is a **supervised** machine learning algorithm that partitions data into groups. It works by learning simple decision rules inferred from the data features to predict the value of a target variable. While commonly used for classification (such as "fruit" vs. "protein"), decision trees can *also* perform regression to predict quantitative values. The algorithm is essentially a flowchart where each node represents a "test" on an attribute, each branch represents the outcome of that test, and each leaf node represents a class label or continuous value to be used as output.

HOW IT WORKS

This family of algorithms works by repeatedly splitting the training data into smaller, more homogeneous subsets until rules for splitting emerge.

- **Attribute selection:** The tree starts at a root node and selects the independent variable that best splits the observations into groups. This is often done using measures like **entropy** (which measures disorder) and **information gain** (which measures the reduction in disorder after a split).
- **Splitting:** A 50-50 split between groups results in maximum entropy (1.0), while a perfectly pure group

has an entropy of zero. The attribute with the highest normalized information gain is chosen for the split.

- **Leaf formation:** This process continues until a termination criterion is met, resulting in leaf nodes that provide the final prediction or classification.
- **Pruning:** To prevent the tree from becoming overly complex and "overfitting" the training data, **pruning** is used to remove branches that provide little predictive power.

What to Use It For

In quality and process improvement contexts, decision trees are highly actionable tools used to partition complex data into simple, interpretable rules for decision-making. Consider using them for tasks like:

- **Process classification:** Determining if a batch of product belongs to a specific quality grade or "group membership" based on measured parameters like temperature or pressure.
- **Predicting quantitative outcomes:** Using regression trees to estimate continuous values, such as predicting the specific yield of a chemical process or a cycle time when the relationship between variables is non-linear.
- **Actionable "if-then" logic:** Creating clear guidance for operators to navigate troubleshooting (e.g., "If the red light is flashing, press the power button twice in rapid succession").

- **Identifying critical factors:** Using "attribute selection" to determine which process variables, such as "sweetness" or "petal length," provide the highest "information gain" and should be prioritized for monitoring.
- **Segmenting outcomes:** Grouping process results into homogeneous clusters to understand why certain sequences of activities result in defects while others succeed.

HOW TO USE IT

Decision trees are intuitive models that mimic human logic by splitting data into branches based on feature values. Build and evaluate one by following the steps below.

Step 1: Prepare Your Data

Decision trees are robust but require clean input. Start by handling missing values through imputation or removal. While trees handle both numerical and categorical data well, many libraries (like Python's scikit-learn) require you to convert categories into numbers. Unlike many other algorithms, you generally do not need to scale or normalize your features.

Step 2: Check Assumptions

The primary assumption is that your target variable *can* be partitioned into distinct groups. Unlike linear models, decision trees do not assume a linear relationship between variables or a normal distribution of residuals. However, be wary of high variance—trees tend to "memorize" noise in the training data, leading to overfitting.

Step 3: Fit the Model

You can use statistical software like R, spreadsheet tools in Excel or Google Sheets, or AI assistants like Claude, Gemini, or ChatGPT. Write a prompt asking the AI to generate regression code and interpret the results (see Figures M4.1 and M4.2 for examples). Always verify that the AI interpreted your data and instructions correctly. Consider re-running your analysis using multiple AI assistants or having one judge the output of another to catch any issues that might arise from the stochastic nature of the assistant.

> I have a dataset about customer churn for a telecom company that includes these variables: tenure: months as a customer (0-90), MonthlyCharges: monthly bill amount (\$18-\$360), Metro: NYC, DC, Pittsburgh, Detroit, Boston, Contract: none, month-to-month, one year, or two year, TechSupport: yes or no, ChurnedMonth: the month that they left the company (0-90), ChurnSoon: yes or no (this is what I want to predict).
>
> Using the following 1000 observations in the attached CSV file, write Python code to build a decision tree classifier using that data that has maximum 3 levels. Visualize the tree, show the feature importances, and explain what the tree reveals about churn patterns and the actions we should consider.

Figure M4.1 A prompt to claude.ai (Opus 4.5) to request a decision tree on sampled data.

MODEL PERFORMANCE

The decision tree achieved **61.7% accuracy** with balanced precision for both classes. This dataset has a notably higher churn rate (48.1%) than typical telecom data.

FEATURE IMPORTANCES

Contract 0.447
MonthlyCharges 0.261
Tenure 0.160
TechSupport 0.132
Metro 0.000

Contract type is the dominant predictor in your data. Metro location has no predictive value in this dataset.

KEY CHURN PATTERNS

By Contract Type (very strong gradient):

- No contract: **70.7%** churn
- Month-to-month: 60.2%
- One year: 41.6%
- Two year: **24.6%** (lowest)

Figure M4.2 Results from prompting claude.ai (Opus 4.5) to build a decision tree.

By Tech Support:

- Without support: 56.5% churn
- With support: 38.6% churn (18 percentage points lower)

By Tenure:

- New customers (0-12 mo): **68.1%** churn
- Loyal customers (48+ mo): 44.0% churn

By Monthly Charges:

- Low ($18-100): 35.9% churn
- Premium ($250+): **60.8%** churn

By Metro:

- Pittsburgh: 55.3% (highest)
- Boston: 41.6% (lowest)

HIGH-RISK SEGMENT

Customers with no/month-to-month contracts + no tech support + <12 months tenure have an **83.9% churn rate**—nearly 4x higher than the low-risk segment (22.0%).

Figure M4.2 Results from prompting claude.ai (Opus 4.5) to build a decision tree. (continued)

RECOMMENDED ACTIONS

1. **Prioritize contract conversion:** The 46 percentage point difference between no-contract and two-year customers is your biggest lever
2. **Bundle tech support aggressively:** Offer free or discounted tech support to new customers—it reduces churn by nearly 18 points
3. **First-year intervention program:** Target customers in months 1-12 with proactive outreach; this is when 68% are at risk of leaving
4. **Price-value communication:** High-bill customers need to understand their value; consider loyalty perks for premium tier
5. **Regional focus:** Investigate Pittsburgh and DC operations—they have materially higher churn than Boston

Figure M4.2 Results from prompting claude.ai (Opus 4.5) to build a decision tree. (continued)

INTERPRETING RESULTS

Interpretation is where decision trees shine. You can visualize the final model to see exactly which features were most influential, and use the tree to explain the model's decisions to stakeholders.

- **Root node:** The most important variable used for the first split.
- **Leaf nodes:** The final prediction points, where your "outputs" appear.
- **If/then rules:** These decisions characterize the branches. For instance, a rule might state that if a food's sweetness is 3 and its crunchiness is 6, it is classified as a "vegetable."
- **Feature importance:** A score indicating which variables contributed most to the model's accuracy. Metrics like "attribute usage" tell you which features are doing the heavy lifting in your model.

Look at summary statistics for your decision tree to see how many cases were misclassified during testing (e.g., "1 error out of 10 cases" or 10.0%). In the output plot, there may be bar charts displayed at the leaf nodes. A "pure" node will be dominated by a single class, indicating a strong prediction.

LIMITATIONS AND PITFALLS

Overfitting: Decision trees can easily become too complex, fitting the noise in the training data rather than the signal. Use pruning or Adjusted R^2 (for regression) to manage this.

Instability: Small changes in the data can lead to a completely different tree structure. Techniques like boosting (generating several trees and using a voting procedure) help mitigate this.

Normalization: While trees can handle various data types, normalizing (scaling) your data can sometimes improve performance, especially in smaller datasets.

Greedy approach: The algorithm makes the best choice at each step (the "greedy" choice) but does not guarantee the globally optimal tree.

METHOD 5

Random Forests

DESCRIPTION

Random forest is a **supervised** machine learning algorithm that builds a "forest" (an *ensemble)* of decision trees to improve prediction accuracy and control for overfitting. Unlike a single decision tree that might be swayed by noise or quirks in your data, a random forest *combines* the outputs of many individual trees, typically through averaging for continuous values or majority voting for categories, to reach a more stable and reliable conclusion. This method is highly effective for finding complex, non-linear relationships between process inputs (predictors) and outputs. Because it uses many trees trained on different subsets of data, it is much more robust than individual models and can handle large datasets with numerous variables without requiring extensive data preprocessing.

HOW IT WORKS

Random forests operate on the principle that multiple expert opinions are more valuable than just one. Examples include:

- **Bootstrapping:** The algorithm starts by creating multiple random subsets of your historical data.
- **Random subsets of variables:** At each "split" in a tree where a decision is made, the algorithm only considers a random selection of predictors. This prevents any single strong predictor from dominating every

tree, allowing the model to uncover hidden patterns in "noisy" data.

- **Aggregating:** For its final prediction, the model averages the results of all individual trees. This "squashes" the errors of individual trees, balancing deviations and generalizing more effectively to new, unseen data.

Use this method when you suspect the relationships in your process are complex or non-linear, or when you have many potential variables and aren't sure which ones are truly important.

WHAT TO USE IT FOR

In quality improvement contexts, consider random forests for:

- **Identifying critical to quality (CTQ) factors:** Determining which machine settings, material batches, or environmental conditions *truly* drive defects, even when those factors interact in complex ways. Using a random forest is an excellent way to identify these factors because the algorithm naturally calculates "feature importance" showing which variables have the most significant impact on the final outcome.
- **Predicting equipment failure:** Forecasting if or when a machine might fail based on a combination of sensor data, maintenance history, and run-time metrics.
- **Optimizing yield:** Finding the "sweet spot" for process parameters where multiple variables must be balanced simultaneously to maximize output.

- **Classifying defects:** Automatically categorizing types of product defects based on image data or multi-sensor readings.
- **Classifying tickets:** Automatically categorizing work tickets based on urgency, content, or triage criteria.

HOW TO USE IT

Step 1: Prepare Your Data

Gather historical observations including your target outcome and predictors. While random forests are more forgiving of outliers and missing values than linear regression, you should still aim for a clean dataset with a healthy number of observations relative to your predictors to avoid overfitting.

Step 2: Visualize Your Inputs

Although random forests are robust against extreme values, you should still examine scatterplots for recording errors or "impossible" data points. A single massive error can still affect splits in individual decision trees.

Step 3: Check Assumptions

While random forests are more flexible than linear regression, you must still verify specific characteristics of your training data to ensure the model suits the problem. Before creating your model, verify:

- **Data representativeness:** Ensure your training data covers the full range of process conditions you expect to see in the future. Because random forests *cannot* reliably extrapolate, the model will struggle to predict outcomes for input values outside the range of your initial sample.

- **Target leakage:** Check that your predictors (inputs) do not include information that would only be known *after* the outcome has occurred. For example, if you are predicting a defect rate, ensure you aren't accidentally including a "post-inspection" metric as an input.
- **Sample size and diversity:** Aim for a dataset large enough to capture the complexity of the process. While there is no strict rule on how many observations you need per predictor, random forests require enough varied examples to grow diverse trees and avoid overfitting.
- **Independence of observations:** Ensure your data points are independent and not influenced by a hidden time-based trend. In quality environments, if one batch affects the next (autocorrelation), the random forest may perceive a relationship that isn't actually driven by your process variables.

After building the model, examine a plot of residuals (the differences between predicted and actual values) which should show random scatter. If you see a distinct curve or a shape like a funnel or horn, your model may be inconsistent across your data range and you might not have a viable model.

Step 4: Fit the Model

You can use statistical software like R, spreadsheet tools in Excel or Google Sheets, or AI assistants like Claude, Gemini, or ChatGPT. Write a prompt asking the AI to generate regression code and interpret the results (see Figures M5.1 and M5.2 for examples). Always verify that the AI interpreted your data and instructions correctly with a human expert, or ask a different AI assistant to evaluate the solution on your behalf.

> Attached is a CSV file with manufacturing data. The target is Quality_Pass (1=pass, 0=fail). Write Python code to load the data, build a Random Forest classifier, evaluate performance, extract feature importance, and provide plain-language interpretation to help a quality engineer to explain the results to a supervisor or senior leader.

Figure M5.1 A prompt to Gemini 3 to build and evaluate a random forest.

Performance Summary

- **Overall Accuracy: 88%** (The model correctly predicts the quality outcome in nearly 9 out of 10 cases).
- Top 3 Quality Drivers:

1. **Material Moisture %** (Most critical factor)
2. Cooling Time
3. Melt Temperature

Leadership Summary: Interpretation of Results

To help explain these findings to a supervisor or senior leader, here is a plain-language breakdown of what the data is telling us:

1. **Material Quality is the Primary "Red Flag"** - The most significant predictor of whether a part will pass or fail is the **Material Moisture Percentage**. This suggests that our pre-processing or drying stage is the most critical point of failure. If the moisture isn't controlled, the likelihood of a quality rejection increases significantly, regardless of how well the machine is running.

Figure M5.2 Results from prompting Gemini 3 to build and evaluate a random forest.

2. **Process Stability Over Operator Influence** - Interestingly, the **Operator Shift** (Day vs. Night vs. Evening) had almost **zero impact** on quality outcomes. This is good news—it means our quality issues are likely "systemic" (caused by physics and materials) rather than "human-centric" (caused by different training or performance levels across shifts). We should focus our engineering efforts on machine settings rather than operator retraining.
3. **The "Big Three" Process Variables** - Beyond moisture, the physics of the mold—**Cooling Time, Melt Temperature, and Injection Pressure**—are the levers we can pull to improve yields. Small fluctuations in these areas are more likely to cause a "Fail" than the age of the machine or the ambient humidity in the factory.
4. **Model Reliability and Next Steps** - The model is currently very good at confirming "Good" parts (high Precision for Pass). However, it is still learning how to catch every single "Fail."

Figure M5.2 Results from prompting Gemini 3 to build and evaluate a random forest. (continued)

- **Recommendation:** We should investigate the specific "Fail" cases that the model missed to see if there is a secondary factor (like a specific raw material batch) not captured in this dataset.
- **Action Plan:** Prioritize an audit of the material drying process and consider automated moisture sensors to flag high-risk batches before they enter the injection hopper.

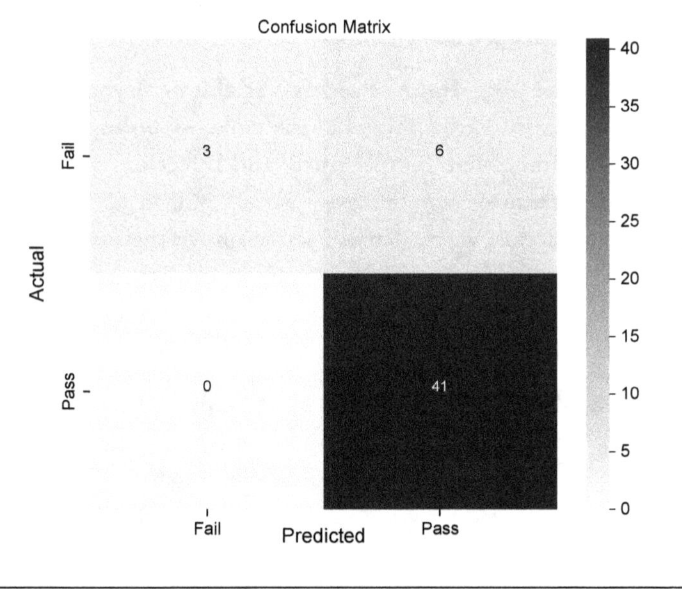

Figure M5.2 Results from prompting Gemini 3 to build and evaluate a random forest. (continued)

INTERPRETING RESULTS

Feature importance: This is the most popular way to evaluate a random forest. It tells you which variables are the biggest "levers" for influencing the output variable.

R2 and mean squared error (MSE): Like linear regression, R^2 tells you how much of the outcome is explained by the model. Lower MSE indicates a "tighter" model with more accurate predictions.

Out-of-bag (OOB) score: A high OOB score means the model performed well on data it didn't "see" during training, giving you confidence in its real-world application.

LIMITATIONS AND PITFALLS

Overfitting: If you have too many trees or too little data, the model might "memorize" the noise in your historical records instead of learning the underlying process.

Extrapolation is bad: Like all models, random forests are unreliable when predicting outcomes for inputs far outside the range of your historical data.

The "black box" problem: While a relationship represented by a single line is easy to read and interpret, a forest of 500 trees is *impossible* to visualize. You gain accuracy but lose some simplicity in explanation.

Root cause risk: Despite the strengths of the method, random forests *can not* be used to reliably find the root cause for an outcome or event.

METHOD 6

Gradient Boosting

DESCRIPTION

Gradient boosting is a **supervised** machine learning algorithm that, similar to random forests, uses an ensemble method. It builds a stronger predictive model by combining a sequence of "weaker" models, typically small decision trees. Unlike linear regression, which finds a single best-fit line, gradient boosting builds a better model iteratively. Each new tree focuses specifically on correcting the errors made by the previous trees, diagnosed by evaluating the residuals.

This method captures complex, non-linear mathematical relationships between inputs (predictors) and outputs. It is a powerful tool for estimating outcomes for new, unseen inputs because it can handle messy, real-world data that isn't linear.

HOW IT WORKS

Gradient boosting works through an iterative process of "boosting" model accuracy using the following techniques:

- **Initial guess:** The algorithm starts with a simple baseline prediction, often the average of all known outcomes.
- **Calculating residuals:** It calculates the difference between the actual observed value and the current prediction (the error).

- **Sequential learning:** A new decision tree is trained to predict those errors rather than the original outcome.
- **Updating the model:** The new tree's predictions are added to the previous model, usually scaled by a "learning rate" to prevent overfitting.
- **Repetition:** This process repeats hundreds or thousands of times, with each step nudging the model closer to the true value until errors are minimized.

WHAT TO USE IT FOR

In quality and process improvement contexts, gradient boosting is ideal for complex systems where variables interact in ways that aren't obvious. These can include:

- **Predicting process outcomes:** Estimating high-stakes metrics like chemical yields or assembly line cycle times where temperature, humidity, and raw material quality interact unpredictably.
- **Identifying non-linear drivers:** Determining which process variables influence quality when the relationship is more complex.
- **Importance analysis:** Identifying which factors matter most in a "noisy" environment where linear models fail to detect the signal.
- **Forecasting defect rates:** Handling large datasets of process parameters to predict the likelihood of defects before they occur.

HOW TO USE IT

Step 1: Prepare Your Data

Collect historical observations including the outcome and potential predictors. Aim for a robust dataset; while simple models work with 15–30 observations per variable, gradient boosting thrives on larger datasets. But unlike linear regression or clustering, gradient boosting can handle missing values and doesn't require "one-hot encoding" for all categorical data.

Step 2: Select a Type of Gradient Boosting

XGBoost, LightGBM, CatBoost, and Gradient Boosting Classifier/Regressor (from Python's scikit-learn) all provide types of gradient boosting. If you have many categorical features with high cardinality (lots of categories to choose from), CatBoost handles these natively without manual encoding and often outperforms the others in this scenario. LightGBM also has categorical support, but XGBoost requires you to encode categorical variables as quantitative variables yourself.

If your dataset is very large (millions of rows), LightGBM is typically fastest, XGBoost is slower, and CatBoost falls somewhere in between. If you have a small dataset, the differences matter less, and you might even prefer scikit-learn's implementation for simplicity, or CatBoost, which tends to be more resistant to overfitting out of the box. Despite its name, CatBoost works great on purely quantitative (numerical) data. The "Cat" in CatBoost refers to its specialized handling of categorical features, but that's an additional capability, not a requirement.

Step 3: Check Assumptions

Before creating your model, verify:

1. **Representative training data:** If your inputs don't reflect what the model will encounter in deployment, your model is doomed to fail. A distribution shift between training and inference is a common cause of model failures in practice.
2. **Sufficient sample size:** Gradient boosting is powerful but prone to overfitting. With too little data, you'll fit noise rather than signal, and your validation metrics won't generalize.
3. **Independence of observations:** Violating this assumption leads to optimistic cross-validation estimates.
4. **Feature quality:** While gradient boosting is robust to many data issues, it can't overcome fundamentally flawed inputs. Encoding errors, mislabeled categories, or outliers representing data errors will propagate through the model and degrade predictions.

Addressing these assumptions can help ensure your model will work when deployed, rather than just *appearing to work* during development.

Step 3: Fit and Tune the Model

You can use statistical software like R, spreadsheet tools in Excel or Google Sheets, or AI assistants like Claude, Gemini, or ChatGPT. Write a prompt asking the AI to generate regression code and interpret the results (see Figures M6.1 and M6.2 for examples). Always make sure AI interprets data and instructions correctly.

> Attached is customer churn data. Write Python code using CatBoost to build a gradient boosting model for which customers will churn, then evaluate how well the model performs, and provide an interpretation of what steps the model suggests we take in practice to reduce churn.

Figure M6.1 A prompt to Gemini 3 to build a gradient boosting model.

> ***Model Performance Evaluation***
>
> Based on the training run, the model achieved the following performance metrics:
>
> - **Accuracy**: 62%
> - **ROC-AUC Score**: 0.646
> - **Precision (Churners)**: 0.55
> - **Recall (Churners)**: 0.60

Figure M6.2 Results from prompting Gemini 3 to build and evaluate a gradient boosting model.

The model shows a solid ability to distinguish between churners and non-churners, with **Contract Type**, **Monthly Charges**, and **Tech Support** being the primary drivers of the prediction.

Interpretation and Practical Steps to Reduce Churn

Based on the feature importance analysis and data distributions, here are the recommended steps for the business:

1. PRIORITIZE LONG-TERM CONTRACTS:

- ✧ **Insight**: Customers with "None" or "Month-to-month" contracts have a churn rate of 60-70%, while those on two-year contracts only churn at a rate of 24%.
- ✧ **Action**: Offer discounts or loyalty rewards to migrate customers from month-to-month plans to one- or two-year commitments.

2. INCENTIVIZE TECH SUPPORT ENROLLMENT:

- ✧ **Insight**: Customers without Tech Support are significantly more likely to churn (56% churn rate) compared to those who have it (38%).

Figure M6.2 Results from prompting Gemini 3 to build and evaluate a gradient boosting model. (continued)

- ✧ **Action**: Include Tech Support as a standard feature in higher-tier plans or offer a "first month free" trial of Tech Support to help customers resolve early friction points.

3. **FOCUS ON EARLY RETENTION (TENURE):**

- ✧ **Insight**: Tenure is a high-importance feature. Customers are most vulnerable to churning in their early months.
- ✧ **Action**: Implement a "New Customer Success" program, reaching out with onboarding assistance or check-ins during the first 3-6 months of service.

4. **MONITOR HIGH-SPENDING CUSTOMERS:**

- ✧ **Insight**: Monthly charges are a strong predictor. High bills without corresponding perceived value lead to churn.

Action: Identify customers in the highest charge buckets and proactively offer them "plan optimization" reviews to ensure they are on the most cost-effective plan for their needs.

Figure M6.2 Results from prompting Gemini 3 to build and evaluate a gradient boosting model. (continued)

INTERPRETING RESULTS

Feature importance: This tells you which variables were most useful for making predictions. If 'Temperature' has a high importance score, it is a primary driver of your outcome.

Mean absolute error (MAE) or **root mean squared error (RMSE):** Use this to understand the average "miss" explained in the same units as your output (e.g., "The model is off by ±2.5 pounds on average").

LIMITATIONS AND PITFALLS

Consider the following potential issues:

Black box: Gradient boosting is harder to explain to stakeholders than a simple equation. You can see *that* a variable is important, but explaining "why" is more complex than just pointing out a single coefficient.

Association vs. causation: Like regression, a high-performing gradient boosting model shows *association*, not necessarily that one factor causes another. Be careful if you're seeking a root cause.

Overfitting: If the model is too complex (too many trees or trees that are too deep), it can predict historical data *perfectly* but fail to satisfy operational needs.

Extrapolation: Like linear models, gradient boosting is unreliable when predicting values outside the range of the training data. Don't try to do that!

Computational cost: Training these models requires more processing power and time than a simple linear regression. If a comparable linear model performs well enough for your needs, there's no need to deploy a more powerful model into production.

Sensitivity to noise: While robust, extreme outliers in the *target* variable can still negatively influence the sequential learning process.

METHOD 7

K-Means Clustering

DESCRIPTION

Clustering is an **unsupervised** machine learning technique: it automatically groups similar items together without being told what to look for in advance. Unlike classification, clustering discovers structure and group membership on its own by examining patterns in your data. It's like asking a colleague to sort a pile of customer feedback tickets into logical groups. You don't need to tell them how many piles to create or what categories to use, because they will examine the content and find natural groupings based on similarity. Some tickets might cluster around delivery complaints, others around product quality, and still others around pricing concerns.

The power of clustering lies in its ability to surface hidden segments that human analysts might miss, especially when dealing with high-dimensional data containing dozens or hundreds of variables. A manufacturing engineer might never think of segmenting machines by the specific combination of temperature variance, vibration frequency, and cycle time that predicts maintenance needs, but clustering algorithms can find exactly these patterns.

HOW IT WORKS

- Clustering algorithms operate on a fundamental principle: items that are similar in measured characteristics likely share underlying causes, behaviors, or outcomes (like the saying "birds of a feather flock together").

- The algorithms work by defining and optimizing *similarity* or *distance*. The K-means approach iteratively assigns points to the nearest cluster center, then recalculates centers based on current members, repeating the process over and over until group assignments stabilize. This process maximizes similarity within a cluster while minimizing similarity between clusters.
- Distance metrics quantify how "far apart" two observations are in the feature space. Euclidean, straight-line distance ("as the crow flies") is most common, but other metrics include Manhattan distance (where you can only move in perpendicular directions, like walking on streets or avenues) and Hamming distance (the "distance" between words or strings).
- The choice of distance metric profoundly affects results. If you're clustering customer transactions, treating a $10 and $10,000 purchase as equivalently "one unit different" from their neighbors would distort findings. Proper scaling and metric selection ensure the algorithm measures similarity in ways that align with business meaning.

WHAT TO USE IT FOR

Clustering excels in situations where you suspect meaningful groups exist but cannot define them in advance. It answers the fundamental question: "What natural segments exist in my data, and what characteristics define each group?" In quality improvement contexts, consider clustering for:

- **Customer segmentation:** Identifying distinct customer types based on purchasing behavior, demographics, and engagement patterns to enable targeted marketing and service strategies.
- **Defect pattern analysis:** Grouping quality issues by root cause characteristics to prioritize corrective actions and allocate engineering resources effectively.
- **Process behavior modes:** Discovering that a manufacturing process operates in distinct "modes" that require different control strategies or indicate equipment degradation.
- **Supplier categorization:** Segmenting vendors based on performance, risk, and strategic value to optimize supply chain management approaches.
- **Anomaly detection:** Identifying outliers that don't fit any cluster—often the most interesting findings for fraud detection, equipment failure prediction, or quality control.

Avoid clustering when you already have well-defined categories and labeled historical data. In these cases, you should use classification instead. If your goal is to predict rather than to segment into groups, regression or time-series methods will be more appropriate. Clustering also struggles when meaningful groups genuinely don't exist in the data, or when all observations are roughly equally different from one another.

HOW TO USE IT

Step 1: Prepare Your Data

Gather historical data. Clean it, handle missing values, and check for outliers and extreme values which can distort cluster centers and boundaries.

Step 2: Standardize and Encode

Because k-means works using distance and similarity measures, it has to operate on numerical data. Standardize quantitative values to z-scores to protect your solution against sensitivity to scale. (Failing to do this causes variables with larger numeric ranges to dominate results, regardless of their actual importance.) Use "one-hot" encoding to turn categorical values into numbers. For example, High/Medium/Low could be recoded to three columns: Level_High, Level_Medium, and Level_Low, where a 1 would indicate whether that value was the selected category, and a 0 would indicate that it was not.

Step 3: Check Assumptions

K-means assumes spherical clusters of similar size. Real data often violates these assumptions. Choosing the wrong algorithm for your data structure produces misleading results. Before creating your model, also verify:

- **Numerical variables only:** K-means uses distance-based measurements to determine similarity between data points.
- **No noise or outliers:** K-means is sensitive to outliers, which can distort cluster centroids and cluster assignments.
- **Variables on the same scale:** Standardize data (typically -1.0 to 1.0) or normalize it (0.0 to 1.0) so the algorithm treats all attributes equally rather than being dominated by variables with larger ranges.
- **No collinearity:** Highly correlated variables are redundant since they represent the same underlying characteristic, essentially adding noise rather than useful information for segmentation.

Step 4: Choose the Number of Clusters

You need to tell k-means how many clusters to look for. One way to do this is to rely on domain knowledge or business requirements that naturally define how many segments make sense for your use case. For a data-driven approach, use the elbow method: run k-means with increasing values of k and plot the **within-cluster sum of squares** for each. Look for the "elbow" point where adding more clusters yields diminishing returns in variance reduction. This bend typically indicates the optimal number of clusters.

Step 5: Fit the Model

You can use statistical software like R, spreadsheet tools in Excel or Google Sheets, or AI assistants like Claude, Gemini, or ChatGPT. Write a prompt asking the AI to generate regression code and interpret the results (see Figures M7.1 and M7.2 for examples). Always make sure AI interprets your data and instructions correctly.

> Attached is a CSV file containing manufacturing data. Standardize the quantitative variables by transforming them to their z-scores and use one-hot encoding for the categorical variables. Write and execute Python code to perform k-means clustering, using the Elbow method to determine the best number of clusters. Provide summary statistics on cluster centers and interpret model results to generate guidance on how to interpret and apply the results in a practical setting.

Figure M7.1 A prompt to Gemini 3 to request a k-means clustering solution.

> ***Clustering Analysis***
>
> Using the **Elbow Method**, the Within-Cluster Sum of Squares (WCSS) was calculated for 1 to 10 clusters. Based on the plot, an "elbow" is visible around **k=4**, suggesting that dividing the data into 4 groups provides a good balance between model simplicity and data representation.

Figure M7.2 Results from prompting Gemini 3 to carry out k-means clustering.

Interpretation of Clusters

Based on the cluster summaries, we can identify distinct operational patterns:

- **Cluster 0:** High quality (96.5% pass), characterized by high injection pressure and shorter cycle times.
- **Cluster 1: The "Failure" Group.** This cluster has a 0% quality pass rate. It is notably associated with the highest average Material_Moisture_Pct (~11.0%) and higher Mold_Temp_C. This suggests that moisture control is a critical factor in product failure.
- **Cluster 2:** High quality (98.7% pass), featuring the highest Melt_Temp_C (~235.6 C) and the youngest machines.
- **Cluster 3:** 100% quality pass, with the longest Cooling_Time_Sec and Cycle_Time_Sec, suggesting a "slow and steady" approach yields the most consistent results.

Practical Application & Guidance

1. **Identify "Red Zones":** Since Cluster 1 captures all the failed parts, the conditions associated with this cluster (specifically high material moisture and specific temperature ranges) should be set as "alert" thresholds in your production monitoring system.

Figure M7.2 Results from prompting Gemini 3 to carry out k-means clustering. (continued)

2. **Process Optimization:** Cluster 3 shows that longer cooling times correlate with perfect quality. You can perform a cost-benefit analysis to see if the increased quality from longer cycle times outweighs the reduced throughput.
3. **Machine Maintenance:** Cluster 2 shows that younger machines are performing well at higher melt temperatures. Older machines (found in Cluster 0 and 1) might need different parameter settings or more frequent maintenance to match this performance.

- **Operator Training:** By looking at the Operator_Shift distribution, you can see if certain shifts are more prone to falling into the "Failure" cluster (Cluster 1). In this dataset, the "Night" shift has a higher count in the failure cluster (21) compared to Day (13) and Evening (10), suggesting a need for focused training or environmental adjustments during night shifts.

By monitoring which cluster a new production run falls into in real-time, you can predict quality outcomes before the part even leaves the mold.

Figure M7.2 Results from prompting Gemini 3 to carry out k-means clustering. (continued)

INTERPRETING RESULTS

Cluster centroids: Examine the center point of each cluster, which represents the average value of all data points in that cluster for each variable. Centroids reveal the defining characteristics of each segment and help you understand what makes each cluster distinct.

Cluster size and distribution: Review how many data points fall into each cluster. Highly imbalanced clusters may indicate outliers forming their own group, a bad choice for number of clusters, or genuinely uneven natural groupings in your data.

Within-cluster variation: Assess how tightly grouped the points are within each cluster. Lower values indicate more cohesive, well-defined clusters where members are similar to each other.

Between-cluster separation: Evaluate how far the clusters are from one another. Well-separated clusters with clear boundaries suggest meaningful segmentation.

Variable importance per cluster: Identify which variables differ most between clusters. Variables with values significantly above or below the overall mean in certain clusters are the key drivers that define and differentiate those segments.

Silhouette score: Use this to measure how well each point fits within its assigned cluster compared to neighboring clusters. Scores range from -1 to 1, where values closer to 1 indicate well-matched assignments.

Before finalizing your analysis, give your clusters meaningful, memorable names that capture their essence. "Cluster 3" tells stakeholders nothing; "High-Volume / Low-Margin Accounts" or "Preventive Maintenance Champions" immediately conveys character and suggests appropriate responses. Good names make it easier for stakeholders to understand (and apply) your results.

LIMITATIONS AND PITFALLS

Forcing clusters that don't exist: Clustering will *always* produce groups, even when data is uniformly distributed. Low silhouette scores or unstable assignments signal potential lack of true structure.

Including irrelevant features: Every variable influences the distance calculation. Including features unrelated to your business question dilutes meaningful patterns.

No ground truth: Unlike supervised learning, there's no objective "right answer" to validate against. Multiple reasonable solutions may exist, and selecting among them requires judgment.

Treating clusters as permanent: Customer segments evolve, process conditions drift, and market dynamics shift. Periodically revalidate your clustering model to ensure continued relevance.

Over-interpreting small differences: Statistical separation doesn't guarantee business significance. Focus on differences large enough to warrant distinct strategies.

METHOD 8

Data Reduction With PCA

DESCRIPTION

Principal component analysis (PCA) is an *unsupervised* machine learning technique for reducing high-dimensional data into a smaller set of uncorrelated variables called principal components. It works by identifying the directions (components) along which your data varies most, allowing you to capture the essential information in fewer variables while discarding noise. PCA is particularly valuable when you have many correlated measurements and need to simplify your data for visualization, analysis, or input into other models.

HOW IT WORKS

- Principal component analysis (PCA) finds new axes (principal components) that are linear combinations of your original variables. The first component captures the most variance in your data, the second captures the most remaining variance (while being perpendicular to the first), and so on. Each component is defined by loadings, which are weights that show how much each original variable contributes to that component.
- This method works because correlated variables share redundant information. By rotating your data to align

with directions of maximum variance, PCA separates signal from noise.

- The components of PCA can be used as inputs to other models. For example:
    - ✧ For each observation in your dataset, PCA calculates a "score" on each principal component. If you started with 20 sensor measurements and reduced to 3 components, each batch now has 3 scores instead of 20 values. These scores are new variables you can use just like any other measurements.
    - ✧ Feed the component scores directly into your downstream model. For example, if you're trying to predict defect rates:

Original approach: Defect rate = f(sensor1, sensor2, sensor3, … sensor20)

After PCA: Defect rate = f(PC1 score, PC2 score, PC3 score)

WHAT TO USE IT FOR

For applications in quality, consider PCA for:

- Simplifying sensor data
    - ✧ Reducing many correlated sensor readings to a few meaningful indices

    - ✧ Creating composite quality scores from multiple measurements
    - ✧ Identifying which sensors provide redundant information

- Detecting anomalies

    - ✧ Building multivariate control charts using principal component scores
    - ✧ Identifying batches that deviate from normal patterns across many variables simultaneously

- Understanding sources of variation

    - ✧ Discovering whether variation comes primarily from materials, equipment, operators, or environmental factors
    - ✧ Revealing hidden groupings in your data that correspond to different process conditions

- Preparing data for other models

    - ✧ Removing multicollinearity before regression (or other) analysis

- Reducing dimensionality (a large number of potential predictor variables) to improve model training speed and stability
- Creating uncorrelated inputs for neural networks or clustering algorithms

When you need interpretable components that use only *some* of the many variables you have available, consider sparse PCA. Sparse PCA forces most variable weights to zero, so each component depends on just a handful of original variables, making it easier to understand what each component represents. When relationships are non-linear, consider kernel PCA or autoencoders. These methods can capture more complex mathematical patterns in your data that standard PCA would miss, since regular PCA only finds linear combinations of variables.

HOW TO USE IT

Step 1: Prepare Your Data

Gather measurements across multiple variables for each observation. Check for missing values and outliers because PCA is sensitive to both. Standardize variables (for example, by converting them to z-scores) when they use different units or scales.

Step 2: Decide How Much Information to Keep

The goal of PCA is to simplify your data without losing the "story" it tells, like summarizing a five hundred-page book into a five-page executive summary. You want to keep enough detail to make good decisions but remove enough noise to see the big picture. To decide how many PCA components to keep (the new summarized categories in the book summarization example), use these three approaches:

- **The "elbow" test:** Look at a *scree plot*, which is a line chart showing how much information each new component adds. Usually, the first few components capture a lot of information, and then the line flattens out. Stop at the "elbow" point right before the line flattens out.
- **The 80% rule:** You want to retain enough components to explain 80% to 90% of the total variation in your data. This ensures you've captured the vast majority of what's happening in your business or market while still significantly reducing the complexity.
- **The "explains more" rule:** Only keep components that provide more information than a single original variable would. If a component explains less than what one of your raw data points did, it's not worth the extra complexity.

Step 3: Check Assumptions

Before creating your model, verify:

- **Linearity:** PCA captures *linear* relationships between variables. If your data has important nonlinear structure, PCA will miss it (consider kernel PCA or other nonlinear methods instead).

- **Magnitude of values:** PCA is sensitive to variance, so variables on larger scales will dominate the principal components. Standardize data unless the original scales are meaningful and comparable.
- **Adequate sample size:** You generally need more observations than variables for stable estimates. With high-dimensional data and few samples, PCA can overfit to noise.
- **Outliers:** PCA is sensitive to outliers and extreme values can distort principal components substantially.
- **Missing data:** Standard PCA can't handle missing values directly. Make sure you handle them in some way in advance, for example by creating values that could potentially be present using imputation methods.

Step 4: Fit the Model

Use statistical software like R, Python, or AI assistants. Write a prompt asking the AI to perform PCA and explain the loadings (see Figures M8.1 and M8.2). Examine which original variables load heavily on each component to give them meaningful interpretations. Always verify that the AI interpreted your data and instructions correctly.

Here is manufacturing data with 5 measurements across 20 batches. Perform PCA to reduce dimensionality. Prepare a Scree Plot (or Elbow Plot) to suggest how many components to keep. Return the explained variance for each component, the loadings matrix, and interpret what each retained component represents in a way that would make sense to a business leader or stakeholder.

The data is:
hardness = (45,52,48,55,47,51,49,53,46,50,54,48,52,49,51,47,53,50,46,55)
density = (2.1,2.4,2.2,2.5,2.2,2.3,2.2,2.4,2.1,2.3,2.5,2.2,2.4,2.2,2.3,2.1,2.4,2.3,2.1,2.5)
tensile = (320,385,340,410,330,365,345,390,315,355,400,335,380,350,360,325,395,360,310,405)
thickness = (1.02,0.98,1.01,0.97,1.03,0.99,1.00,0.98,1.04,1.00,0.96,1.01,0.98,1.00,0.99,1.02,0.97,1.00,1.03,0.96)
moisture = (5.2,4.8,5.1,4.6,5.3,4.9,5.0,4.7,5.4,5.0,4.5,5.1,4.7,5.0,4.9,5.2,4.6,5.0,5.3,4.5)

Figure M8.1 A prompt to claude.ai (Opus 4.5) to reduce data using PCA.

Dataset Overview

- 20 batches, 5 measurements per batch
- Variables: Hardness, Density, Tensile Strength, Thickness, Moisture

Explained Variance by Component

PC1: Eigenvalue 5.14, explains 97.70% of variance (cumulative: 97.70%) PC2: Eigenvalue 0.08, explains 1.59% of variance (cumulative: 99.28%) PC3: Eigenvalue 0.02, explains 0.39% of variance (cumulative: 99.67%) PC4: Eigenvalue 0.01, explains 0.22% of variance (cumulative: 99.89%) PC5: Eigenvalue 0.01, explains 0.11% of variance (cumulative: 100.00%)

Loadings Matrix

Hardness: PC1 = +0.448, PC2 = +0.293, PC3 = +0.721, PC4 = -0.426, PC5 = -0.109 Density: PC1 = +0.445, PC2 = +0.556, PC3 = -0.651, PC4 = -0.262, PC5 = +0.034 Tensile: PC1 = +0.450, PC2 = +0.209, PC3 = +0.155, PC4 = +0.842, PC5 = +0.148 Thickness: PC1 = -0.446, PC2 = +0.569, PC3 = +0.065, PC4 = +0.201, PC5 = -0.658 Moisture: PC1 = -0.447, PC2 = +0.489, PC3 = +0.166, PC4 = -0.041, PC5 = +0.729

Figure M8.2 Results from using claude.ai (Opus 4.5) to execute PCA.

Component Retention Recommendation

Based on the scree plot analysis, the recommendation is to **retain 1 component**. PC1 alone captures 97.7% of the total variation in your data, which exceeds both the 80% and 95% thresholds commonly used. The scree plot shows a sharp "elbow" after PC1, with all subsequent components contributing negligible variance.

Business Interpretation of PC1: Material Quality Index

PC1 represents a composite measure of overall material robustness and quality. All five measurements load onto this component with nearly equal weight, but in two opposing groups.

- **Positive contributors** (move together): Hardness (+0.448), Density (+0.445), and Tensile Strength (+0.450). When these values increase, PC1 increases.
- **Negative contributors** (move in opposite direction): Thickness (-0.446) and Moisture (-0.447). When these values increase, PC1 decreases.

In practical terms, batches with high PC1 scores have stronger, denser material with higher tensile strength, combined with lower thickness and lower moisture content. These represent your premium-quality output. Conversely, batches with low PC1 scores have softer, less dense material with higher moisture and thicker profiles.

Figure M8.2 Results from using claude.ai (Opus 4.5) to execute PCA. (continued)

Loadings Matrix

Hardness: PC1 = +0.448, PC2 = +0.293, PC3 = +0.721, PC4 = -0.426, PC5 = -0.109 Density: PC1 = +0.445, PC2 = +0.556, PC3 = -0.651, PC4 = -0.262, PC5 = +0.034 Tensile: PC1 = +0.450, PC2 = +0.209, PC3 = +0.155, PC4 = +0.842, PC5 = +0.148 Thickness: PC1 = -0.446, PC2 = +0.569, PC3 = +0.065, PC4 = +0.201, PC5 = -0.658 Moisture: PC1 = -0.447, PC2 = +0.489, PC3 = +0.166, PC4 = -0.041, PC5 = +0.729

Component Retention Recommendation

Based on the scree plot analysis, the recommendation is to **retain 1 component**. PC1 alone captures 97.7% of the total variation in your data, which exceeds both the 80% and 95% thresholds commonly used. The scree plot shows a sharp "elbow" after PC1, with all subsequent components contributing negligible variance.

Business Interpretation of PC1: Material Quality Index

PC1 represents a composite measure of overall material robustness and quality. All five measurements load onto this component with nearly equal weight, but in two opposing groups.

- **Positive contributors** (move together): Hardness (+0.448), Density (+0.445), and Tensile Strength (+0.450). When these values increase, PC1 increases.

Figure M8.2 Results from using claude.ai (Opus 4.5) to execute PCA. (continued)

- **Negative contributors** (move in opposite direction): Thickness (-0.446) and Moisture (-0.447). When these values increase, PC1 decreases.

In practical terms, batches with high PC1 scores have stronger, denser material with higher tensile strength, combined with lower thickness and lower moisture content. These represent your premium-quality output. Conversely, batches with low PC1 scores have softer, less dense material with higher moisture and thicker profiles.

Key Takeaway for Stakeholders

Your five measurements are highly correlated and essentially capture a single underlying quality dimension. Instead of tracking five separate metrics on dashboards and reports, your team should consider monitoring one composite **"Material Quality Index"** score derived from PC1. This simplifies quality control, makes anomaly detection faster, streamlines batch comparisons, and reduces cognitive load for operators reviewing production data.

Figure M8.2 Results from using claude.ai (Opus 4.5) to execute PCA. (continued)

INTERPRETING RESULTS

Understand your key outputs:

- **Eigenvalues** tell you how much of your data's overall variation each component explains. For example, if you're trying to understand what drives differences in customer behavior, the first component might capture 40% of those differences, the second 25%, and so on. Bigger numbers mean that the component is doing more heavy lifting.

- **Scree plot** shows those eigenvalues in order. Components before the elbow (where the plot flattens out) are worth keeping; those after it are mostly capturing noise rather than meaningful patterns.
- Loadings measure how strongly each original variable contributes to a component, ranging from -1 to +1, where values closer to either extreme indicate a stronger relationship. To interpret what a component means in business terms, identify the variables with the largest absolute loadings (typically above 0.3 or 0.4) and ask what they have in common. That shared theme becomes the component's business label.

    - ✧ For example, if hardness, density, and tensile strength all load positively on PC1, you might call it "material strength." If you're analyzing customer data and a component has high loadings on purchase frequency, average order value, and time on site, you might interpret that component as "customer engagement."

- Loadings close to +1 or -1 mean that variable strongly defines the component. Loadings near zero mean that variable isn't really part of what the component is measuring.

Name your components: Meaningful names that express what the combined variables represent can make results more actionable.

Use component scores: Once you've selected components, you can calculate scores for each observation. These scores become new variables for plotting, monitoring, or feeding into other analyses. Points with extreme scores warrant investigation.

Validate your results: Check that your interpretation makes practical sense. If a component doesn't have a logical explanation, be cautious about using it.

LIMITATIONS AND PITFALLS

Correlation ≠ causation: Like all correlational methods, PCA reveals associations, not causes. Variables that load together may share a common cause rather than directly influencing each other.

Linear relationships only: PCA assumes relationships between variables are linear. (Non-linear relationships require kernel PCA or other specialized techniques).

Scale sensitivity: Without standardization, variables with larger scales dominate the analysis. Always standardize when units differ greatly from each other, or have lots of internal range.

Outlier sensitivity: Extreme values can dramatically distort components. Screen for outliers before running PCA, or use robust PCA methods.

Interpretation challenges: Components are mathematical constructs and may not correspond to intuitive factors that are meaningful to a product or process. Sometimes the most statistically optimal solution isn't the most useful.

Information loss: Discarding components means losing some information. Usually this is exactly what you're aiming for as you reduce your data, but stay aware!

METHOD 9

PRACTICAL NATURAL LANGUAGE PROCESSING (NLP)

DESCRIPTION

Natural language processing (NLP) is a family of techniques that enable computers to understand, interpret, and generate human language. For quality improvement practitioners, NLP makes it possible to extract insights from unstructured text data such as customer feedback, incident reports, and survey responses. This allows you to systematically analyze the vast amounts of text that organizations generate daily but rarely examine in depth, often limited by data acquisition or transformation requirements. AI assistants like Claude, ChatGPT, and Gemini have made NLP accessible without programming expertise. You can now perform sophisticated text analysis by describing the code you need in plain language, making these techniques practical for frontline quality professionals.

HOW IT WORKS

NLP has several core capabilities that quality practitioners can leverage:

- **Sentiment analysis** classifies text as positive, negative, neutral, or mixed. This helps you quickly gauge customer satisfaction across thousands of comments without reading each one individually.

- **Text classification** automatically categorizes text into predefined groups. You can sort customer tickets by issue type, route complaints to appropriate departments, or identify recurring problem themes.
- **Named entity recognition** extracts specific information such as product names, dates, locations, or people mentioned in text. This enables structured reporting from unstructured narratives.
- **Summarization** condenses large volumes of text into key points. Review hundreds of customer comments quickly by generating summaries that highlight the most important themes.

WHAT TO USE IT FOR

In quality improvement contexts, consider NLP for:

- **Voice of the customer analysis:** Transform open-ended survey responses and feedback into quantifiable insights. Identify what customers *actually* complain about versus what you *assume* they complain about. Using systems like Claude Cowork, you can even combine your data with data automatically mined from online and social sources.
- **Incident report mining:** Extract root cause patterns from narrative incident reports. Discover connections between incidents that numerical data alone would miss.

- **Service ticket triage:** Build models that automatically categorize and prioritize incoming requests based on content, sentiment, and urgency signals in the text.
- **Process documentation review:** Analyze standard operating procedures, work instructions, and process documents to identify inconsistencies, gaps, or opportunities for improvement.

HOW TO USE IT

Step 1: Prepare Your Text Data

Gather the text you want to analyze. This might be exported from your ticketing system, CRM, or survey platform, or manually extracted and compiled from documents. Ensure data is in a format you can share with an AI assistant (e.g. CSV, Excel, or plain text). Remove personally identifiable information if privacy is a concern before using public AI assistants. For best results, aim for at least 50-100 text samples when looking for patterns.

Step 2: Define Your Analysis Goals

Be specific about what you want to learn. "Analyze this feedback" is too vague. Better: "Categorize these 250 customer tickets by issue type and identify which categories have the most negative sentiment." Clearer objectives lead to more actionable outputs.

Step 3: Identify Python Packages to Try

You can enhance the performance of NLP executed through an AI assistant by specifically asking it what Python packages you would like it to use when it writes code to carry out your instructions. The most common Python packages for NLP are:

- **spaCy:** The best for production NLP pipelines. Fast, efficient, and comes with pre-trained models for many languages. Handles tokenization, part-of-speech tagging, named entity recognition, and dependency parsing out of the box.
- **Scikit-learn:** Widely used for text classification using TF-IDF vectorizers, naive Bayes classifiers, and other traditional ML approaches to NLP.
- **Gensim:** Includes topic modeling and document similarity including Word2Vec, Doc2Vec, and LDA implementations. Use this to find themes and patterns across collections of documents.
- **Hugging face transformers:** The standard for modern deep learning NLP. Provides access to thousands of pre-trained models (BERT, GPT, RoBERTa, etc.) for tasks like sentiment analysis, text classification, summarization, and question answering.

For a quality improvement practitioner, spaCy offers the best balance of capability and ease of use for tasks like entity extraction from incident reports, while Transformers provides high accuracy for sentiment classification if you need more precision.

Step 4: Craft Your Prompt

Write a prompt that explains your data structure, desired output format, and specific analysis tasks. Be sure to spot check your analysis, or ask a second AI assistant to serve as judge of the first one to evaluate your results.

See the examples below for guidance on effective prompts. Prompt 1 is provided (Figure M9.1) along with a complete response from an AI assistant (Figure M9.2) to show you what is possible. Prompts 3 and 4 (in Figures M9.3 and M9.4) are provided for you to try with your own AI assistants. Have fun exploring!

PROMPT 1: SENTIMENT DISTRIBUTION ANALYSIS

I have customer service ticket data with a sentiment_label field containing values like Positive, Negative, Neutral, and Mixed. Please use spaCy or Gensim to write code to analyze the distribution of sentiment across all 250 tickets and create a summary table showing:

1. Count and percentage for each sentiment category

2. Average CSAT score for each sentiment category (where available)

3. Top 3 recurring subjects for negative sentiment tickets

Figure M9.1 A prompt to claude.ai (Opus 4.5) to request sentiment distribution analysis.

1. SENTIMENT DISTRIBUTION

Sentiment	Count	Percentage
Neutral	105	42.0%
Negative	70	28.0%
Mixed	39	15.6%
Positive	36	14.4%

2. TOP 3 RECURRING SUBJECTS FOR NEGATIVE SENTIMENT TICKETS

Total negative sentiment tickets: 70

1. "URGENT: System completely down"
   - Count: 9 tickets (12.9% of negative tickets)
   - Key themes: access, account, unacceptable
2. "Furious about data loss"
   - Count: 9 tickets (12.9% of negative tickets)
   - Key themes: saved, data, gone

Figure M9.2 Results from claude.ai (Opus 4.5) detailing sentiment distribution analysis.

3. "Worst customer service ever"
    - Count: 9 tickets (12.9% of negative tickets)
    - Key themes: hold, minutes, worst

3. ADDITIONAL INSIGHTS

Categories with Most Negative Sentiment Tickets:

- Returns: 11 tickets
- Technical Support: 11 tickets
- Account Management: 9 tickets

Products with Most Negative Sentiment Tickets:

- Analytics Dashboard: 12 tickets
- Cloud Storage: 11 tickets
- Pro Plan: 9 tickets

4. KEY TAKEAWAYS

- Neutral sentiment dominates the ticket base at 42%, suggesting most customers have routine inquiries without strong emotional reactions.
- Negative sentiment (28%) significantly outpaces Positive (14.4%), indicating room for service improvement.

Figure M9.2 Results from claude.ai (Opus 4.5) detailing sentiment distribution analysis. (continued)

- CSAT scores correlate strongly with sentiment: Positive tickets average 4.71 while Negative tickets average only 1.82.
- The three most common negative issues (system outages, data loss, poor customer service) each account for about 13% of negative tickets, pointing to specific areas needing attention.
- Technical Support and Returns categories, along with Analytics Dashboard and Cloud Storage products, should be prioritized for quality improvements.

Figure M9.2 Results from claude.ai (Opus 4.5) detailing sentiment distribution analysis. (continued)

PROMPT 2: IDENTIFYING COMMON ISSUES

Review the 'description' field in this customer service dataset. Identify the top 5 most common issue themes that appear across tickets, regardless of the existing category labels.

For each theme:

- Provide a descriptive label
- Count how many tickets mention this theme
- Quote 2-3 representative excerpts
- Suggest one process improvement based on this theme

Figure M9.3 A prompt to claude.ai (Opus 4.5) to evaluate themes across tickets.

PROMPT 3: DEEPER ANALYSIS

> Cross-tabulate ticket priority (Low, Medium, High, Urgent) against sentiment_label to answer: Are high-priority tickets *really* the ones with negative sentiment?
>
> Create a matrix showing the count for each priority-sentiment combination. Identify any misalignments where tickets marked Low priority have Negative sentiment, suggesting our triage process may be missing upset customers.

Figure M9.4 A prompt to claude.ai (Opus 4.5) to perform deeper NLP-based analysis.

INTERPRETING RESULTS

Validate against known cases: Before trusting NLP analysis at scale, manually review 10-20 examples to confirm the AI's classifications match your judgment. If sentiment labels don't align with what you'd assign, refine your prompt with clearer definitions or examples.

Look for patterns, not perfection: NLP analysis excels at revealing trends across large datasets. Individual misclassifications matter less than whether the overall patterns are directionally correct. A sentiment analysis that's 85% accurate still provides valuable insights over hundreds or thousands of comments.

Connect text insights to metrics: The most powerful insights come from linking NLP findings to quantitative outcomes. In the customer service data, you might discover that tickets containing words like "urgent" or "deadline" have significantly longer resolution times, revealing a gap between customer expectations and service delivery.

LIMITATIONS AND PITFALLS

Privacy and confidentiality: Text data often contains sensitive information. Use discretion before agreeing to upload customer communications, employee feedback, or proprietary documents to external AI services. Understand your organization's policies—and respect them!

Context matters: Sarcasm, industry jargon, and domain-specific language can confuse NLP analysis. "This product is sick" might be positive slang or a genuine complaint depending on context. Always provide domain context in your prompts.

Garbage in, garbage out: NLP cannot extract insights that aren't present in the text. *If customers write vague complaints like "it didn't work," no amount of analysis will reveal the root cause.* Consider whether your text data contains sufficient detail for meaningful analysis.

Consistency varies: AI assistants may classify similar text differently across separate sessions. For critical analyses, consider running the same prompt multiple times and comparing results, or asking the AI to explain its reasoning for borderline cases.

Representativeness: The text you analyze may not represent your full customer base. People with extreme experiences (very positive or very negative) are more likely to leave feedback. Silent customers may have different concerns entirely.

Watch for category imbalance: If 80% of your text is classified into one category, assignments to smaller categories may be less reliable due to sample size.

Glossary

Accuracy—A performance metric that measures the proportion of correct predictions out of all predictions made. Accuracy can be misleading when one category is much more common than another (imbalanced classes).

AUC-ROC (Area Under the Curve-Receiver Operating Characteristic Curve)—A metric that evaluates how well a classification model distinguishes between categories across all possible decision thresholds. Values range from 0.5 (no better than random guessing) to 1.0 (perfect discrimination).

Classification—A type of supervised machine learning that predicts which category or group an observation belongs to, such as spam/not spam, fraud/legitimate, or high/medium/low risk.

Clustering—An unsupervised machine learning technique that automatically groups similar observations together without being told what categories to use. Useful for discovering natural segments in customer data, defect patterns, or process behaviors.

Coefficient—In regression models, a number that shows how much the predicted outcome changes when a predictor variable increases by one unit. For example, a coefficient of 5.84 for height means each additional inch of height adds 5.84 units to the predicted value.

Confusion Matrix—A table that summarizes a classification model's predictions by showing true positives, true negatives, false positives, and false negatives. Essential for understanding where a model makes mistakes and calculating performance metrics.

Data Drift—A change in the statistical properties of incoming data compared to the data used to train a model. When data drift occurs, model predictions may become less reliable because real-world conditions have shifted.

Decision Tree—A supervised learning algorithm that creates a flowchart of if-then rules to classify observations or predict values. Highly interpretable because you can trace exactly why any prediction was made.

F1 Score—A performance metric that balances precision and recall into a single number, useful when both false positives and false negatives matter. High F1 indicates the model is good at finding true positives without generating too many false alarms.

False Negative—An error where the model predicts "no" when the answer should have been "yes." In medical testing, this means missing a patient who actually has the disease. Also called a Type II error.

False Positive—An error where the model predicts "yes" when the answer should have been "no." In fraud detection, this means flagging a legitimate transaction as fraudulent. Also called a Type I error.

Feature—A measurable characteristic or variable used as input to a machine learning model. Features are the predictor variables that help the model make predictions, such as customer age, purchase history, or temperature readings.

Feature Engineering—The process of creating new predictor variables from raw data to improve model performance. For example, calculating "days since last purchase" from a raw date field.

Gradient Boosting—An ensemble learning technique that builds many simple decision trees sequentially, with each new tree correcting errors made by previous trees. Implementations like XGBoost and LightGBM often achieve high accuracy on structured business data.

Isolation Forest—An unsupervised approach for outlier detection that randomly slices observations into smaller groups until every item is completely by itself. Because normal items are tightly clustered together, it takes a lot of slices to separate them. However, rare items (anomalies) sit far away from the rest of the group and get isolated in just a few cuts.

K-Means Clustering—A popular clustering algorithm that groups observations by repeatedly assigning each point to its nearest cluster center and recalculating centers until groupings stabilize. Requires specifying the number of clusters in advance.

Labeled Data—Training data where each observation includes both the input features and the known correct answer (the label). Required for supervised learning methods like regression and classification.

Linear Regression—A supervised learning algorithm that finds the best straight-line relationship between predictor variables and a numerical outcome. Produces interpretable coefficients showing how each factor affects the prediction.

Logistic Regression—A supervised learning algorithm that predicts the probability of an observation belonging to a particular category (typically yes/no). Despite its name, it is used for classification, not predicting numbers.

Loss Function—A mathematical formula that measures how wrong a model's predictions are during training. The model adjusts its internal settings to minimize this score, learning from its mistakes over time.

MLOps (Machine Learning Operations)—The collection of practices, tools, and cultural approaches that enable organizations to deploy and maintain ML systems reliably at scale. Includes version control, automated deployment, continuous monitoring, and experimentation infrastructure.

Model Drift—The gradual degradation of model performance over time as real-world conditions change from those present in the training data. Requires ongoing monitoring and periodic retraining to address.

Multicollinearity—A condition where two or more predictor variables are highly correlated with each other, making it difficult to determine which variable is actually driving the outcome. Can cause unstable coefficient estimates in regression models.

Natural Language Processing (NLP)—A family of machine learning techniques that enable computers to understand, interpret, and generate human language. Used to extract insights from text data such as customer feedback, incident reports, and survey responses.

Odds Ratio—In logistic regression, a measure of how much the odds of an outcome change when a predictor increases by one unit. An odds ratio of 2.0 means the odds double; a ratio below 1.0 means the odds decrease.

Offline Learning—An approach where a model is trained once on historical data, frozen, and deployed without updating based on new information. Appropriate when patterns are stable and regulatory requirements demand human review before model changes.

Online Learning—An approach where a model continuously updates itself as new data arrives, adapting to changing patterns in near real-time. Useful when conditions shift rapidly, such as in fraud detection or personalized recommendations.

Overfitting—When a model memorizes the specific quirks and noise in training data rather than learning the underlying pattern. An overfit model performs well on historical data but fails to make accurate predictions on new observations.

P-value—A statistical measure indicating whether a predictor variable's relationship to the outcome is likely real or could have occurred by chance. Values below 0.05 typically indicate the relationship is statistically meaningful.

Precision—A performance metric that answers: "Of all the items we classified as positive, how many actually were positive?" High precision means few false positives.

Principal Component Analysis (PCA)—An unsupervised technique that reduces high-dimensional data into fewer variables called principal components while preserving the most important information. Useful for simplifying complex datasets and removing redundant measurements.

R-squared (R^2)—A metric that indicates what percentage of the variation in your outcome is explained by the predictor variables. An R^2 of 0.70 means the model accounts for 70% of the variation, with 30% coming from unmeasured factors or noise.

Random Forest—An ensemble learning method that builds many decision trees on random subsets of the data and combines their predictions. More robust than a single decision tree because it averages out the noise from individual trees.

Recall (Sensitivity)—A performance metric that answers: "Of all the items that actually were positive, how many did our model correctly identify?" High recall means minimizing false negatives, which is critical in medical diagnosis and fraud detection.

Regularization—A technique that prevents overfitting by adding a penalty for model complexity. Ridge regression shrinks coefficients toward zero, while Lasso regression can eliminate unimportant variables entirely.

Sentiment Analysis—A natural language processing technique that classifies the emotional tone of text into categories (such as positive, negative, or neutral) by comparing words and phrases against a reference lexicon that provides standards.

Standardization—A technique to prevent excessive dynamic range in an input variable, often achieved by taking the z-score of the values.

Supervised Learning—Machine learning where the model learns from observations with known correct answers (called "labeled data"). The model discovers patterns that map inputs to outputs, then applies those patterns to make predictions on new data.

Training Data—The inputs that are cleaned, prepared, and (sometimes) standardized to reduce dynamic range within and between predictor variables. This prevents a model from favoring one predictor over another.

Unsupervised Learning—Machine learning where the model identifies hidden patterns or groupings in data without being told what to look for. Used for clustering, dimensionality reduction, and discovering structure in complex datasets.

Z-Score—The number of standard deviations above or below the mean of a collection of data. 95% of observations fall between a z-score of -2 and +2, while 99.7% of observations fall between a z-score of -3 and +3.

www.ingramcontent.com/pod-product-compliance
Lightning Source LLC
LaVergne TN
LVHW010614100826
845148LV00014B/2969

* 9 7 8 1 6 3 6 9 4 2 3 8 4 *